A BURBAGE BOYHOOD

Dennis Perkins

Tales, written from the heart, about my boyhood from 1950 to 1965, up to 14 years of age, whilst living in the village of Burbage in Leicestershire.

Conditions, community, tribulations, and antics.

Lots of old photographs.

TABLE OF CONTENTS

FOREWORD

I have not written this book in order to educate anyone. I merely wanted to share the wonderful and powerful memories of my boyhood in the 1950s, which I spent in Burbage, Leicestershire.

I also thought it would be nice to have a record to pass down through my family. I would have loved a similar book to read if one of my ancestors had written one.

DEDICATION

This book is a brief look at me and my family in the past. However, I have dedicated it to my family of the future.

My Grandchildren, Annabel Mann, Oliver Mann, and Melanie Perkins.

I love you all.

THANKS

- My sincere, heartfelt thanks (in no particular order) go to the following:
- **Paul Gardner of Hinckley District** Past and Present, for his encouragement, when this book began existence as a seventy-five-minute talk given to Local History Groups. Also his wife **Sue** and their wonderful **team of volunteers** who work so hard. Also to Hinckley District Past and Present members everywhere.

- **Sylvia** and **Geoff Whitworth** and **Paul Williams** of Burbage Heritage Group for their encouragement.

- **Deborah** and **Ian Phillpott** of the Hinckley Group of the Leicestershire and Rutland Family History Society for advice on research.

- **Anne Crabtree MBE** and **Phillip Lindley** and the whole team at Hinckley and District Museum for the hard work they do for the residents of Hinckley District

- **My wife** for her tolerance.

ABOUT THE AUTHOR

Dennis Perkins was born in Leicester in 1950. His Boyhood was spent in the Leicestershire village of Burbage. At the age of 14 he moved to nearby Hinckley when his parents bought a small shop. After training, he qualified as a mechanical engineer in 1972 and married in the same year. He remains happily married. He became involved in the quality and safety of mining equipment manufacture. In 1988, he became a quality manager at a world class precision engineering company. In 1991 he started his own business providing consulting services to small businesses and multi-site organisations nationwide. Over the next 25 years he advised many types of company on business laws and also standards for quality, safety, training and the environment. This involved writing many bespoke technical and procedural manuals. He has two grown-up children, a son (born 1977) and a daughter (born 1982). He has a Granddaughter born 2008, a Grandson born 2010 and another Granddaughter (born 2013). He is active in several local groups related to history, heritage, family history research and his local museum.

PROLOGUE: MY BEGINNINGS

The Soldier [December 1950]

The soldier stood, slightly stooped, over the open drawer and cried. His heart seemed to ache physically as he struggled to maintain control of his emotions. A tiny baby, just a few weeks old, lay in the large, open bottom drawer of the tall chest. The baby, wrapped well, was warm and snug. The infant's face twitched, and his eyes blinked as one or two of the soldier's tears fell upon his upturned little face.

The soldier was aware that he MUST go. His short compassionate leave had come to an end, and he knew only too well that he must soon depart, leave behind all those who he loved in Hinckley, Leicestershire, England and return to his posting in Dortmund, Germany. He had no choice but to go, even though he wished with all his heart and with all his soul that he could stay.

A beautiful dark-haired young lady standing nearby, with tears rolling down her cheeks, gently placed her hand on the soldier's arm and whispered that it was time. He turned and looked at her, and she could see the despair harboured in his eyes. They embraced for several minutes. He kissed her tenderly, then, with a last fleeting glance at the sleeping baby, turned suddenly. Crossing the room of the old terraced corner house, he picked up his backpack. He whispered goodbye to a middle-aged lady who stood dabbing at her eyes with a folded handkerchief. He gave her a peck on the cheek as he passed her on his way to the door...

The two women followed him out into the side street, calling their goodbyes and waving. Wiping his eyes with the back of his hand, he walked to the corner of the street. Turning back once for a final wave and a call, he turned the corner and disappeared from their view. Squaring his shoulders, he marched resolutely into the cold, frosty night and headed towards the railway station some half a mile distant.

THE SOLDIER

RAYMOND PERKINS

1929 – 2010

(MY DAD)

Service in Germany

Such was my beginning, for I was the baby, only weeks old. The beautiful young woman was my Mother, Joyce. The middle-aged lady whose rented house we all occupied was my grandmother, Gladys Wright. Sadly, the early death of her husband, Tom, my maternal grandad, at the age of 48, just a few weeks before my birth, meant that we never met. I was born in Leicester on the 22nd of December 1950. This was in early January 1951. World War Two had ended only five years ago. Some things were still on ration. Signs of austerity were still to be seen everywhere. The world had not yet fully recovered from the horrors of this major conflict. I was born into a working-class family. A good family, honest, proud, and tight-knit, but like many others, my parents were living in drab poverty on a soldier's meagre wage with no home of their own, and now they were to be separated again by a soldier's posting.

A few months later, Dad was able to return briefly from his posting with the Royal Engineers and take a few days of break from driving huge Scammel trucks. These massive old articulated trucks with huge platform-type trailers and many wheels were more commonly used for transporting tanks, but in this case, they were used for transporting cranes and other plant required for bridge building. He did not, however, spend his *entire* time helping to rebuild all the bridges the RAF had blown to bits only a few years earlier. The officers soon took advantage of his carpentry skills, and so he was often seconded to make, repair, maintain, and improve the furniture, in common areas, the officer's mess, their offices, and indeed for their own private quarters too.

After Dad's short leave, at the tender age of about six months, I travelled with my parents via train, ferry, and train again to Army married quarters in Dortmund, Germany. We also apparently spent some months in Hanover. My earliest memory is a vague one. Holding on tight to the thick coat of a German Shepherd dog as I straddled its back. It belonged to my Dad. The dog's name was Max. We were living in Germany. I'm sure my Dad must have had a secure hold of me to prevent me from slipping off the dog. In my memory, we were on a red-brown carpet on some sort of landing. We lived in a small flat in British Army married quarters.

When my Dad had served his time in Germany and was to return to England, he could not afford the quarantine and transportation costs necessary to bring Max home. I have always had a soft side to my nature, and I remember crying a couple of years later, back in England, as Mum told me what had happened after I had enquired about what had happened to Max.

Return to Blighty

I was about two years old when Dad was demobbed from the army in 1952 and brought Mum and baby me back to England. Times were tough. We had no house and no money, so we had to go and live with my Gran Wright again. Gran Wright's rented house was at 127 Queens Road, Hinckley, Leicestershire, about a mile from Burbage on the corner at the junction with Princess Street. It was a bit crowded, but no doubt Mum and Dad were grateful. My Mother's eldest brother, Ron, was still serving in the Army in Egypt, but that still left Mum, Dad, and baby me sharing the house with Gran, Mum's other brother, Gordon, and her two sisters, Mavis and Anne. It was cramped, but I don't remember any particular friction between family members.

There was a very small scullery as you entered the back door. The dining area was part of our "living room," on the outer wall of which sat a large black-leaded range that provided the only heating. There were fireplaces in most of the rooms in the house, but I never saw a fire lit in any of them except for the range, even though Gran Wright still lived there until I was about 12 years old. In those days, the front room was kept in pristine condition and order. The only time it was used was when visitors came. Otherwise, it was strictly out of bounds. Between the living room and the front room, an alcove ran under the stairs. It was almost like a short tunnel. On one side, there were useful drawers and cupboards from floor to ceiling. I have a memory from being a toddler of my Mum's youngest sister, Anne, aged about ten years, opening a drawer to show me a still-born kitten. There was also a small piece of floorboard missing which was utilized as a marble hole on rainy days. It was quite a big old house, but right up until the late 1950s, when extensive improvements were made, it had no toilet, no bathroom, no running water, and no electricity.

Until then, we shared our neighbour's toilet. We used a galvanized bath in front of the fire but often also used slipper baths run by Ted Ellis, the Manager of the local swimming baths in Station Road. Otherwise, it was daily strip washes in the scullery. Water was hand pumped from a well into a Belfast sink in the scullery and transported in jugs and saucepans to wherever it was needed. The only lighting was from ceiling-mounted gas lights. One in the living room and one in the front room. Everyone had their own candle holder and candle to take upstairs to bed to emphatic and repeated instructions to ensure that their candle was out before they settled down to sleep. The candles were replenished from a box fixed to the wall on the stairs. There was no spare money and only just enough to pay the household bills and for everyone to eat. Along with thousands of other working-class families at that time, we were down, but we were not out. This was the beginning of life for me, but readers, particularly younger ones, do not be tempted to pity me, for there were millions of people in those post-World War Two times who were in such poverty and worse. I knew nothing else at that time and thought of it as normal. Besides, I was cared for by a loving, happy family and could not have been more content.

Looking up Queens Road. The first house on the left was Gran's in front of the house near that tree.

Gran Wright in her yard standing on a rug sent to her from her eldest son Ron in Egypt, where he was serving with the British Army.

Note the washing mangle, the galvanized bath, and the slab closing off the well.

Family photographs were taken by Mum at the top of Lash Hill late 1940s.

Left to right, Gordon on the fence, Mavis in front of Gran, and to the right, Anne pulling a face and standing in front of my Grandad [Tom].

CHAPTER ONE: HOME SWEET HOME

My Aunt Mavis was always particularly good to me. When I was about four years old, she would collect me, and we would walk about a mile and a half over to Gran Wright's house, where I would be entertained until mid-afternoon and then escorted on the walk back home. I once told my Mum that I loved going to Gran Wright's house "because they have sausages and tomatoes for dinner every day" (we did not call our mid-day meal lunch then. It was always dinner).

At that age, the days of the week meant nothing to me at all. I had assumed that because I had sausages and tomatoes every time I went to Gran's house, they ate it every day. I had not realized that I always went on a Saturday and, therefore, always enjoyed my sausage and tomatoes, unaware that it was their Saturday treat menu and that they did have a varied menu on other days.

A Home of Our Own

After living at Gran Wright's house again for about six months, in 1953, we were allocated a prefab by Hinckley Urban District Council.
It wasn't much to look at, but we lived there from 1953 to 1965. Twelve initially hard, but generally, very happy years.

Prefab Construction

It was a two-bedroom "prefab" designed to help the post-war housing shortage. They were pre-fabricated, then transported, and the panels assembled on site and bolted down onto pre-set concrete bases. They were made from asbestos panels with wooden panels and coated steel panels, containing a thin layer of glass fibre wool for insulation. The windows and doors were steel framed and glazed with single panes of glass. There was only one source of heat. A small, solid fuel burner in the living room. When it was really cold weather, you could sit in front of it, very close to it, until your front was red-hot, but your back would still be freezing cold [this caused a weird sensation]. A hot water bottle warmed my bed for a while before I got in and snuggled down. There were loads of army blankets and coats on top of them if necessary, and often, in the wintertime, I would wake to see that ice had formed on the inside of the windows and the steel frames. I soon learned to wash and dress very quickly, and I would have layers of "woollies" on. Dad had an old sports jacket that he wore around the house all winter, and when spring came each year, it seemed strange for a few days to see him in his shirt sleeves, minus his jacket.

Location

Number 46 Banky Meadow was located directly at the bottom of a steep hill. From the main road leading to the village centre, a turning led you into Woodland Avenue, and in those days, it was indeed a tree-lined avenue. The houses in Woodland Avenue were council houses, traditionally brick-built and semi-detached. About two-thirds the way down the hill, Woodland Avenue ceased and became Banky Meadow, and the houses here were all prefabs, fifty in all. They were built-in lines going off to each side of the road and were only accessible via pedestrian walkways about four feet wide. We called them alleyways.

Each prefab had an Anderson air raid shelter left over from the war, which, bricked up at each end, served as a coal house/shed. Four-foot chain link fences carved up the land so that each prefab had a front and a back garden with a yard at the side.

As you came to the bottom of the hill, you had the choice of crossing the road and entering our own prefab via the front gate. You could also choose to walk pavements or drive on roads to the left or right, both of which ran to dead ends within a few hundred yards. Beyond the road to the left was a large open area of wasteland containing both sand and clay pits. This was referred to by us kids as the "sand'ole" (we never sounded our aitches). Beyond the dead end to the right was a smaller area of wasteland containing quite a few trees and bushes. Beyond that were Farm fields separated from the wasteland by a natural brook and a line of huge well-established trees. The fields were neat and square. Each one was bordered with a 15 inch x 15 inch ditch and a neat three-foot high hedge. At the corners, wooden fences and stiles formed a small, square, fenced area.

Between each prefab were wire fences. Our front garden was lawned, and our back garden was a good size and bordered at the bottom by a hedgerow of assorted trees and bushes. To one side was a huge elm tree. On the other side of the hedgerow was a cornfield. At the top of the hill, there was a large recreation ground with several football pitches and the village team cricket pitch, complete with changing rooms. Tucked away in the corner were swings, see-saws, and two roundabouts. A little further afield were Burbage Woods and Burbage common. All of this was heaven to all the kids who lived in the area. There was plenty of open space for us to roam free, play, and go "scrumping" for apples, pears, and damsons.

I hope I have set the scene. Our "prefab" was initially sparse, drab, and cold, but my parents ensured that I wasn't badly affected. The local surroundings provided me with a fantastic open "playground," so my childhood was happy and carefree. Our prefab was in a perfect location for growing up. From the main road between Hinckley and Burbage, Woodland Avenue branched off to the North East. It was a long hill and carried straight on to Banky Meadow, the long descent continuing to the last row of prefabs. In those days before additional roads crawled over the existing fields, if you lived in a brick semidetached house, you lived on Woodland Avenue. If you lived in a prefab, you lived in Banky Meadow. There was only a jitty through to Sapcote Road.

At the top of Woodland Avenue, across Hinckley Road, there was a recreation ground with swings and roundabouts and a huge expanse of flat, level green ground with football pitches and cricket pitches. Even nearer than that were sandpits, clay pits: fields to roam, trees to Climb: Burbage Woods and common nearby, and several orchards with apple trees, pear trees, and damson trees bearing delicious fruit (or so I'm told). There were ditches, brooks, streams, and ponds, so we had plenty of water to fall into.

Prejudice

It has to be said that there was a stigma about living in a prefab. I came up against blatant prejudice several times and found it very upsetting. In the 1950s, society was obsessed with class, and it seemed to me that everyone had to be pigeonholed. I remember a school teacher once explaining to the class that a manual worker living in his own house is 'Upper Working Class.' A man doing the same job and living in a brick-built council house is Middle Working Class, but a man with the same job living in a prefab is Lower Working Class...... "at best," he added, looking directly at me. I cannot remember what is or was below "Lower Working Class," but it seemed to me that we were pretty near the bottom of the pile. It's true that we were often looked down upon. I have been very careful, ever since, to assess people PURELY by what they say and what they do. I don't really care where they live, or what job they have, or what colour they are, or which church they go to, or anything else. It's about CHARACTER for me.

There were those who derided prefabs and looked down on people who lived in them. However, prefabs came with a built-in refrigerator, an inside toilet, a bathroom, plenty of storage space, a copper [for washing] gas cooker, and a fold-down table in the ample kitchen. Better facilities than many brick-built houses had at that time.

Community

Our local community, particularly in the prefabs, was a poor but friendly one. We were all in the same boat. Money was really tight. Everyone got on with their work and helped others if they could with a loan of the odd culinary item or perhaps child minding whilst someone went to the Doctor – things like that. Discord in our adult community was seldom, and when it occasionally erupted, it was a brief skirmish and soon blew over, and things would quickly settle down back to normality. My mother worked at home doing folding and bagging for the hosiery industry until I started school when she returned to work at the factory for better pay.

Diet

The nutritional value of our diet varied, and sometimes it was not good, but I never went hungry. I don't remember ever feeling hard done by. I knew nothing else. We just got on with life. In the mid1950s, a *typical* menu for our main meal of the day would read something like as follows:-

EARLY 1950s DINNERS

Sunday	Small cheap cut joint, e.g., Shoulder/belly pork, ribs/neck of lamb, roast spuds, and homegrown veg (when available).
Monday	Fried up leftover mashed spud, and sometimes veg [from Sunday]. (Bubble and squeak). Our large steel frying pan crisped it up, and I loved it. If you were lucky, you might get a small portion of bacon or meat, leftovers from Sunday breakfast and lunch, respectively.

Tuesday	Lamb breast/ribs. These had about 3 mm of lean meat running along each bone and 10 mm of crisped-up fat running around the edge or sometimes homemade soup with bread and butter.
Wednesday	Corned Beef Hash, sometimes with peas or sometimes Cheese and Onion Pie with homemade chips.
Thursday	Tripe and onions or sometimes egg and homemade chips, sometimes with a fish finger or two or a rasher of bacon. Occasionally a roast lamb's heart.
Friday	A sandwich before cubs/scouts and a bag of chips from the chippy afterward, sometimes with a pickled onion, always with batter bits.
Saturday	Sausage and tomatoes at Gran Wrights.

We often ate the food then that has completely gone "out of fashion" Such things now are generally met with negative comments from the younger generation who find the thought of eating offal 'disgusting' or 'gross' whereas cheaper food such as tripe, lamb's heart, pigs Trotters, faggots, chawl, kidneys, liver, brawn, black pudding and dripping were enjoyed and helped to fuel us and put less strain on our food budget.

Our first house and happy home. 46 Banky Meadow, Burbage.

This is what my Mum and Dad looked like when my Burbage Boyhood began.

This is what I looked like as my Burbage Boyhood began.

The living room in our prefab.

Note the St. Michaels black and white TV and our lovely sideboard standing on linoleum. I still have that clock. Going by flowers and cards, it's Mum's birthday.

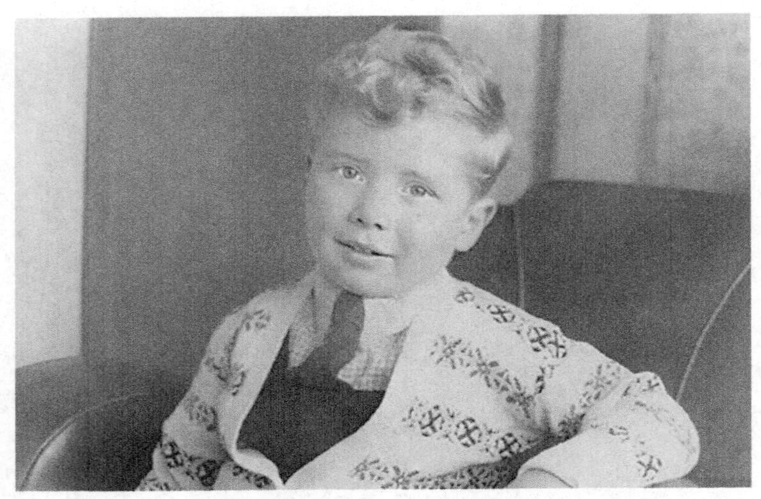

Me in our living room on my favourite armchair

Dad relaxing in our yard.

Note the coalhouse made from an Anderson Air Raid Shelter left over from the war. Early re-cycling from Hinckley Urban District Council.

CHAPTER TWO: PEOPLE

I used to love to be at Gran Wright's old house, but I would hate it as a child when Gran lit the gas light as the evening shadows were falling. She would pull the brass chain on one side of the lamp to open the gas valve. [The chain on the other side closed the gas valve]. The whooshing sound of the gas was quite loud and immediately put me on edge.

"Hurry up and light it, Gran," I would plead, suddenly feeling very tense.

"Alright," she would say with mild irritation. She would then wander over to the black leaded range upon which she kept a brass jug containing her spills.

"Please hurry, Gran." By now, I was lying in a quivering heap on the sofa.

"I am doing," she retorted as she sorted through her spills. Some were too short of reaching the gas mantles up inside the globe and were only of a suitable length to light Gran's Woodbines. [cigarettes].

"Hurry up, Gran, light it, light it." After about three days, she would find a spill to her liking and poke the end into the range fire until it burst into flame. She would then shield it with her other hand like a candle to prevent it from going out and walk very slowly back to the gas lamp, which had been whooshing gas out for some time now.

"Gran, you'll blow us up, light it, Gran, light it. She would casually raise the hand holding the spill, and there was a flash of flame and a sudden BOOM. I would involuntarily clutch at my chest where I imagined my heart to be, jump high in the air, and land on my back

on the sofa, where I needed a few moments of gasping and groaning to recover.

Although this operation traumatized me every time, Gran didn't bat an eyelid and always raised her eyebrows in surprise at my reaction as she walked back to the range to distinguish the spill and replace it in the brass jug.

This picture is NOT of my Gran nor her house, but it shows Gas Lighting.

Family

Over the next decade, the considerable efforts of my parents achieved improvement for us. Our diet gradually improved, and so did the interior of our prefab until it was like a little palace. New linoleum and carpets were saved, along with a new light bowl. A lick of paint and wallpaper in the best room made all the difference. A few years after we moved in, the council painted doors and window sills/frames and coal houses, previously all dark green. They were transformed with fresh, bright colours, light blue, royal blue, light green, and red, in order as they worked along the row. The metalwork on our prefab became red. A large paraffin heater and electric bed warmers now made the winters more comfortable.

My Dad kept on trying to better himself and earn more money. From boot and shoe operative, he got a better job driving a Commer truck for Nuneaton Flour Mills. He would have to carry bags of flour weighing one hundredweight (1 cwt = 112 lbs) on his back and toss them onto his truck until he had the correct number of bags for the run neatly stacked and safely roped on the flatbed. He would usually load and drive between 1 and 4 runs a day, depending on the distance travelled.

He told me that one day he was driving with a full load (probably overloaded) down a hill near Furnace End in Warwickshire when his brakes failed. With lights full on and horn blaring, he careered down the hill with the handbrake pulled on fully, both feet on the brake pedal, pulling up on the steering wheel for extra force. He sped by a stationary van missing an oncoming car by an inch, and after several other near misses, managed to come to a halt, engage crawler gear and switch off the engine. Beads of sweat stood on his forehead, and he was so stiff from the fright he had a job to release his hold on the steering wheel and dismount from the cab.

He walked 3 miles to find a telephone kiosk and rang his boss. He and the truck were recovered and returned to Nuneaton Depot. By this time, it was well into the afternoon. He was sent on a short run in another truck and docked half a day's pay because the first load did not get delivered. He left and became a tipper truck driver for the Wharf Concrete Company located at the side of the canal in Hinckley. The wharf was originally built to load and unload narrow boats.

It would be about 1955 after my Uncle Ron had been demobbed from the army and returned from Egypt to England. He needed to earn some money, so my Dad put in a word with the boss and got him a job as a driver's mate. After a few weeks, Dad's usual "mate" left the company, and he was teamed up with a new Driver's Mate – Guess who? Yes – Uncle Ron. They worked together very well. Why wouldn't they? They had always got on together. However, there was one day when they had a few short sharp words for each other. For some time, Dad had been telling Ron not to slam the door so hard when he jumped out of the cab. Ron could not get out of this habit formed during his army service. One day as he jumped out of the cab, he slammed the door and the glass shattered. My Dad was technically in charge of the vehicle and Uncle Ron, so he had a few words to say, and afterward, they both had a telling-off from the wharf manager. However, it was soon forgotten.

My Mum also did everything she could to maximize her contribution to the family finances and well-being. She contacted her previous employers and carried out several different operations for them as an outworker. She worked very hard in between her relentlessly ongoing tasks, such as making sure that our home was always clean and tidy and our meals were ready on time. She also made sure that we all had suitable clothes ready on time for work/school/playing etc.

I recall the Foreman from the factory bringing her work from his vehicle to the house. He would often comment and compliment her because the work he had previously left was always ready for him. Our bathroom was full of heavy gauge cotton bags containing stockings, but the bags were soft and came in handy as a makeshift bed when visitors wanted to sleep over.

Mum was also the money manager. Everything was cash in those days, and she devised her own system for making sure that our bills were paid. She had an envelope for every expense, even ad-hoc items. Written on the envelopes were the minimum amounts of cash she had to put in every week to ensure that we could pay everything at the right time and the total cash amount actually saved in the envelope. Gas, electricity, coal, rent, one item only on HP [such as a small table or a paraffin heater], shopping [still referred to as rations, a throwback to the war]. Co-op savings bank for clothes, especially for school or Sunday school sermons and later our holidays. She used this system all her life.

Their support for me was given unconditionally, even though the first consideration was always financed. "I would like to go swimming lessons, Mum," or "I want to join Cubs." "How much are the swimming lessons, and will you need bus fare?" and "Don't apply to join Cubs just yet. I'll let you know when." I knew that she would need a bit of time to determine costs and organize money for a uniform etc. But go swimming lessons and join Cubs etc. I certainly did.

If I got a game of football in the school team or played a part in a Cub/Scout Pantomime, I entered the high jump at the school's sports day, or when I took part in the annual Sunday school treats parade around town. At least one of them would try to be there to support me, and if at all possible, both of them, and if circumstances were right, sometimes they would bring along other family members, particularly Aunt Mavis and my Grandparents.

MY FAMILY TREE [Correct During the Period 1950 To 1965 Covered By This Book]

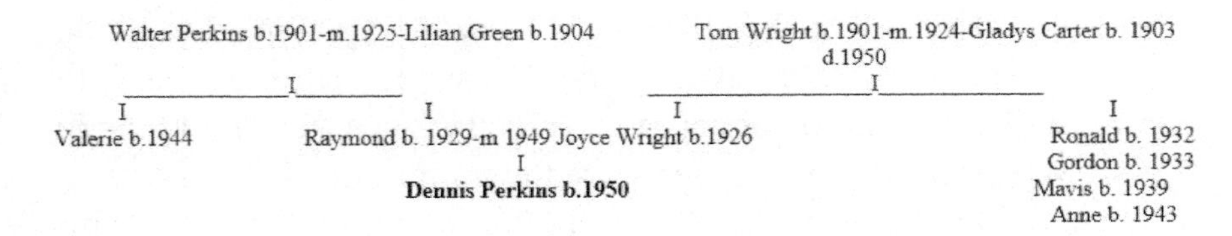

Walter Perkins, my Paternal Grandfather

Walter lived in Earl Shilton, Leicestershire, all of his life. He worked as a Clicker in the boot and shoe trade. This was the top skilled job cutting the leather to the correct shape. The name "Clicker" was taken from the sound the machine made. He used to tell me really corny jokes, and I loved them. He was very useful with a cue and was good at billiards and snooker. He also sang in the Earl Shilton male-voice choir for years and had a beautiful deep, resonant voice. He used to sing along with a radio program, very popular at the time, called 'Sing something simple'. I used to love to hear him. He loved a regular beer or two but only drank in moderation at the Lord Nelson Inn and the "Stute" [Earl Shilton Institute]. I never ever saw him worse for a drink.

He was quite tall, of a medium slim frame, and was deceptively strong. He did not swear and would fit other words in where other people may have sworn, for example, "That *blinking* referee is a *thumping* idiot." He was quietly spoken, and he never raised his voice, but everyone seemed to listen to him when he spoke.

We used to go on long walks together. He was very keen on nature and would point things out to me, like trees, animals, and birds. Our walks would often end up with me in a pub yard with a bottle of Vimto and a packet of crisps while Grandad slipped into the bar for a quick pint. He was a good gardener too. He grew fruit and made jam. His specialties as a gardener were chrysanthemums and also tomatoes which were delicious. He would often bring 'Gran Lil' on the bus to Hinckley, then catch another to Burbage and arrive just in time for tea. He was always interested in what I was doing or playing or learning at school. I always felt close to him, and I was really upset when he died aged 68 when I was 18. I really missed him.

Lilian Perkins [nee Green], My Paternal Grandmother

I called her Gran Lil. She came from Barwell. Several of her family, especially her Dad, did very well at cricket. Unfortunately, her Dad, Isaac Green, died in 1920, aged 43, and Lil's mother died in 1922, aged 44, leaving Gran Lil as the eldest to look after her four younger siblings when she herself was only just turned 17 years old. She had to fight very hard to stop the authorities from taking the younger ones into care. Her youngest sister, Florence [known as Nance], was only two years old. They had a very hard time of it, but she was determined to keep them together and eventually, they all grew up and, one by one, got married and moved on.

Despite her early hardships, Gran Lil was a very jovial individual. She used to laugh through clenched teeth and make a funny shish shish noise. She saw the funny side of things very easily and laughed a lot. She was quite short, and as she got older, she put on weight and became very round. Before she had my Dad, she also worked in the boot and shoe industry, and that is probably how she met Walter.

Gran Lil was particularly close to her sister, Edna, and they would spend lots of time together at each other's houses and going for a game of Bingo which Gran Lil liked to do. They would also go on holiday together at various British seaside resorts. She was about 66 years old when she lost her beloved Walter. She had been married to him for 45 years. She lived on for 29 years and passed away in 1998, aged 94.

Valerie Perkins, My Dad's Only Sister [My Aunt]

My Dad's sister. I was always close to her. We spent time together when we were young. There were only seven years of gap between us, and we always got on. We both spent lots of time with my Mum's siblings, Gordon, Mavis, and Anne. We didn't see so much of Mum's eldest brother Ronald [always known as Ron] because he was away a lot serving with the Army, mainly in Egypt. But when he was there, he was certainly one of 'the gang,' and we all had great times together. I was an only child, and they became the brothers and sisters that I never had. I loved them all.

I would often spend time with Val at Earl Shilton when staying with my Grandparents, Walter and Lil. Valerie was a good piano player, and of course, being a music lover from an early age, I loved to hear her play. I used to pester her all the time, asking her to play for me. However, I don't recall a single instance of her becoming irritable. My favourite was a piece called 'The Maiden's Prayer' written by Polish composer Tekla Bądarzewska-Baranowska, which was published in 1856 in Warsaw. If I stayed over, a makeshift bed would be made up in the corner of Valerie's bedroom, but again she never seemed to mind me being there. We would giggle and whisper in the dark. She had often been to the cinema with friends and would tell me all about the film she had been to see.

Val always said that she never really knew what Raymond, her brother, as well as a brother and sister, should have done. When Val was born, my Dad was 15 years old, and by the time Val could walk and talk, Raymond was in Germany serving with the Royal Engineers, during which time he got married and left the Perkins family home in Earl Shilton. It's true to say that they clashed at times. However, they were typical of so many siblings and were there for each other, without question, if needed.

Raymond Perkins, My Dad

A family man. Strived constantly and persistently to better himself and improve life for his family. He retrained several times from being a Carpenter, then Soldier, Lorry Driver, Boot and Shoe Operative, Hosiery Knitter [Mekker], Shop Keeper and Engineer. With Mum's help run a shop [open seven days a week] whilst at the same time working what was known as Three Eight Hour Shifts. This involved working as a hosiery knitter for a week of 'Mornings' [0600 to 1400 HRS] followed by a week of 'Afternoons' [1400 to 2200 HRS] followed by a week of 'Nights' [2200 to 0600 HRS] on a continuous rota.

He was an even-tempered, steady, reliable, patient man but could erupt with anger if put out. This was not often. Members of the family knew they could go to him for help and often did. He was particularly close to his Dad, Walter, and was devastated when Walter died in 1969.

He was a very keen freshwater Angler from an early age and loved Nature. He got into trouble quite a few times for playing truant from school to go fishing. He would tell me tales of having breakfast and then walking a couple of miles to a local lake and then walking back, in the early evening, fishing tackle on his back, up Shilton Hill, tired and starving, not having had a bite to eat since his breakfast cereals.

He told me quite a few tales of when he was a boy, like when he was delivering papers around Earl Shilton when he was about 15 [1944], and a German plane jettisoned a stick of bombs just as he looked up. As they hung in the air, he thought they were coming straight for him, so he dived behind a wall and lay there scared as hell. In the event, this was an optical illusion, and they landed on waste ground behind a row of houses, causing no real damage except for a huge crater. No one was hurt.

Another time they heard a plane flying very low over the recreation ground opposite their house. The plane's engine was spluttering. "Don't worry, that's one of ours," said Grandad. **BOOOM**! The German plane dropped a bomb on the far side of the field.

He also told me that his Dad, Walter, once caught him smoking in the huge sandpit at the back of their house.

Thomas Wright, My Maternal Grandfather

Always known as Tom, he was my maternal Grandfather. He was born in Nuneaton. His family came from Lichfield in Staffordshire. His parents had moved down from Lichfield in Staffordshire shortly before he was born. His father was a railway plate layer, and I suspect that he moved down to Warwickshire for work. He found a job as a miner, then later a quarry worker, and the family settled in Stockingford. He was on the team of workers who dug out [by hand] the locally famous 'Big Pit' [now re-filled]. Thomas died in 1950, aged 48, just a few weeks before I was born, so I never got to meet him.

Gladys Wright [nee Carter], My Maternal Grandmother. I stayed at Gran Wright's house a lot from being born up to when I got married at the age of 21 [1972]. It was a happy house despite the sadness of losing Grandad Wright so early. Gran had a radio. It was wooden, and it was massive. 40 cm wide x 40 cm breadth x 60 cm high. It had a lovely speaker providing a loud, clear wonderful tone once it was properly tuned. With no electricity in the house, it ran off an accumulator [large chargeable battery]. I remember having to take it around the corner to a little shop to get it charged. I think it cost two [old] pence [0.8 new pence] and lasted about a week, depending on the use, of course.

Gran spoke old Hinckley. I Shernt cook till later. I Can't be doing wi all that. That car backfiring FRIT me te death. I allus do me washin on Mondeh. Instead of saying, "I knew that lady," she would say, "I knowed er." Also, there were no H's at the beginning of words. Burbage and Hinckley people have a distinctive way of pronouncing the end of words ending in Y. She was Appeh to live in Inkleh, walking on the courseh with the famileh.

She had loads of funny sayings. In the morning, she would draw back the curtains saying, "I'll let God's light in........ it's cheaper than ours." If something was neither one thing nor the other – she would say, "Well, that's neither charcoal nor watercress." During bad weather, she would look out of the window and say, "The poor dickybirds ain't got much to sing about today."

I remember, as a toddler, asking Gran about my Grandad, who died suddenly, aged only 48, just before I was born. She would talk to me about him, and I would become sad that I never got to meet him. Gran soon put me right. She said, "Well, look ere me duck, we are all borned [old Hinckley speak], and we all atter [have to] die, there are no exceptions." To me, at that age, this was 'clear, concise, and unquestionable wisdom' passed on in one sentence. She was old-fashioned, yet in some ways, she was before her time. Long before the Rolling Stones ever sang the song, she made it very clear to me, "You can't always get what you want."

During my visits to, and stays with, Gran Wright, as I grew older, I made friends with some of the local kids. Traffic levels were low, and Princess STREET, as it was then, was a dead end. This was years before they continued the road around to Priesthills Road to become Princess ROAD.

Roy Rogers at Gran Wrights

Us kids, playing in Princess Street when it was a dead end

I recall lorries reversing along Princess Street to load up with the big skips used in those days in the hosiery trade to and from the Manchester Hosiery factory. I particularly remember Bees Transport because of the "Bee" logo painted on the side of the lorry. The other one I particularly remember was Walter King Transport. Walter King's son, Tom King from Burbage, was such a nice chap, and he always made us kids laugh. Sometimes the drivers would chat with us kids while they were waiting, and if we were lucky, we might get a sweet or a biscuit from the cab. Things were different then. Occasionally, a driver would even have a kick-about with us.

Joyce Perkins [nee Wright], My Mother

My Mum, Joyce, was the oldest daughter, then Ron, then Gordon, then Mavis, then Anne, was the youngest. As I look back, my Dad's sister, Valerie, was nearly always there too. As an only child myself, these people to me were the brothers and sisters that I never had. I loved them all, and they all loved me. They gave their time freely and willingly, and if I did occasionally need someone, then at least one of them would be there as if by magic.

On Gran Wright's doorstep, Back Row left to right; Mum, Gordon, Mavis.

Front Row left to right; Anne, me with Teddy, and Valerie.

The Wright family left to right; Ron, Mum, Anne, Mavis, and Gordon

My parents were devoted to each other. My Mum was a very complex character. She was nervous and had phobias about going out, going into strange buildings and even traveling, especially on buses or trains, due to claustrophobia. She had some sort of inferiority complex too and was worried about what people were thinking of her and the family. In contradiction to all that, she had a dominant side to her nature and got involved with situations within the family, often getting stressed out herself. She always meant well but would often get agitated. Some of this was no doubt connected to her Dad's early death. Being the eldest child, she had always felt it her duty to look after the others. Despite her concerns and worries, she was proud of the whole family and would defend us all from outside criticism. She could stand up for herself if someone annoyed her. She and Dad were absolutely and totally devoted to one another.

Ron Wright, My Mother's Eldest Brother. [My Uncle]

I didn't see so much of Ron as I did his siblings. He served abroad for a long time in the Army. When he was on leave or had free time, he would often visit us and always had a present for me in his bag. He would insist on taking me out while he had the chance. I have a memory of him visiting us when I was a toddler. Out of the bag came my present. In this instance, it was a lovely warm blue winter suit. He took me for a walk, and I was repeatedly sniffing as I had a bit of a cold. We went into a shop for some sweets, and I began to sneeze. He quickly went to the fruit section. Oranges in those days came in wooden boxes in layers separated by shaped cardboard. In addition to that, each orange was wrapped in orange tissue paper with a trademark on it. "You need some vitamin C," explained Ron. "Four should do it." By the time the shopkeeper had put the oranges in a paper bag, Ron had four orange tissues to wipe my nose for me. It's funny what we remember. In the 1950s, he married a girl from South Wales and went to live with her in the city of Newport and found work in the steelworks there. Later on, in life, I was to become really close to Ron, but that's another story.

Gordon Wright, My Mother's Youngest Brother. [My Uncle]

Gordon was very ill as a baby. He suffered from more than one illness, the details of which I know not. I do know he ended this run of illnesses with Yellow Jaundice. He was a weak and sickly child, to begin with, but very gradually recovered. He was small like his Mother, Gladys, but worked for years for Dunkley's, a local shop and bakery. He worked on the vans, delivering bread and groceries all over Hinckley and District in all weathers, carrying loads. The days were long, and he worked very hard. Whilst he was by no means stupid, he was a little slow, and perhaps because he grew up in a home full of only women [Mother and sisters], he always sounded slightly effeminate.

He also spent time with me when I was a child, and we got on very well. He was good to me. He was very thrifty with money. One of his little idiosyncrasies was that if anyone asked him to contribute to something, he would do so but with much muttering and moaning and tut-tutting. However, the funny thing was that if HE thought of treating someone or of buying them a present, he could be very generous.

Mavis Wright, My Mother's Eldest Sister. [My Aunt]

Mavis was always very good to me. We have always been close. Of all the family, she spent the most time at our prefab and the most time looking after me, spending time together and going to places and doing things together. We would walk in the local parks, go for bike rides and visit the cinema [South Pacific and Westside Story spring to mind]. In her youth, she loved dancing, particularly ballroom dancing. She had a crowd of friends who she would meet up with regularly at local dance venues like 'The George' and 'Leo and Annabelle's.

Occasionally, a boyfriend would appear with her for a while, but things never seemed to get serious enough to last long. I remember, in particular, a Terry who drove a green Triumph TR2 sportscar and an Eric who was a really nice chap.

When my Dad worked in the Hosiery Industry, he would be on nightshift every third week. As Mum was of a nervous nature, Mavis would sleep over at our prefab on those weeks. Dad was on 'nights,' so I would see her from tea-time through the evening and when I woke up. She would often appear at weekends, so I saw a lot of her on those days.

Anne Wright, My Mother's Youngest Sister. [My Aunt]

Anne was the youngest of the family, and just like Val, she was only about seven years older than me. She visited us at our prefab but not so often as Mavis. However, when I went to stay at Gran Wright's house, she never objected to me tagging along with her as she played with her mates. They were happy for me to be included and got to know me and were friendly toward me too. I particularly used to enjoy hide and seek on dark nights at the time. I was not old enough to be out on my own in the dark. So, for instance, when I was seven, Anne would be fourteen, and we would both hide together in the pitch-black night, say between a brick wall and a shed in someone's back garden. It was so exciting trying to be quiet so as not to get found. Anne met her husband-to-be, Arthur, whilst we were living in Burbage. He was also good to me and would play football or indoor games with me.

Friends and Neighbours

My very first Burbage Pal was a little girl over a year younger than me. I have a very clear memory of me, as a toddler, sitting in the back garden of our prefab in Burbage. I am sitting on the earth in our back garden on a warm day and digging into the soil with a seaside spade. I was about two and a half years old. I was close to and facing a four-foot-high chain link fence and just on the other side of the fence was one of my earliest childhood Burbage friends. Her name was Dawn, and she was only about 22 months old. She was doing the same as me, and sometimes we would both stop digging and talk to each other. How much of these conversations would have been understood by an adult is hard to tell in the present day, but we were happy to spend time together digging away and sometimes finding worms to stretch and attempt to tie in a knot. A bond was formed, and we remained friends until her family moved to another area, I think, in the late 1950s.

My first car and first girlfriend

I was a quiet, shy little boy. Almost timid. I wouldn't say boo to a goose. I always backed off and tried to avoid trouble. I never stood up for myself. Consequently, I was pushed around and bullied quite a lot. Mum got so fed up with me coming home with "shiners" [facial bruises, especially under the eye] that she used to actively encourage me to hit kids back. Dad tried to help by giving me boxing lessons in our kitchen. Unfortunately, during one demonstration, he punched a hole in the kitchen wall. Boy, was he in trouble when Mum came home and saw the damage. It made me laugh, though. Anyway, Mum and Dad's efforts were all in vain. I totally lacked any aggression.

I always looked after Dawn. She was one of the youngest, smallest, and most vulnerable of the huge gang of thirty-odd kids who lived in Banky Meadow and Woodland Avenue. I don't really know why I looked after her. I wasn't asked to. I wasn't told to. I just did. One day when I was five years old, a local bully boy who did not live in Woodland Avenue or Banky Meadow, some two years older and much bigger than me, suddenly appeared whilst Dawn and I were playing on the road just outside our front gardens. His name was Gary. He pushed me roughly two or three times. I was scared, and each time he pushed me, I tried to turn away. This went on for some time. He punched me hard in the ribs. I winced and then did what I always did. I backed away.

Then, Gary made a mistake. A big one. He pushed little Dawn right over into some shrubs. A little girl half his size. I was furious, and without even thinking about it, I launched myself at him. There wasn't much boxing going on. Dad's lessons had been wasted on me. My arms were whizzing round like propellers rotating at the elbow. He landed three jabs to penetrate through my propellers. The first one hit my chin and stunned me a bit, but I kept going. The second hit my nose, and it poured blood all over my white shirt. I just kept punching away. The third caught me high on my cheekbone, and my eye immediately began to close up. My propelling arms splattered blood from my nose everywhere, including over both of us. I was outraged that he had tried to hurt Dawn, and for once, I kept punching, on and on until, eventually, I was slowly moving forward, arms flailing like a windmill, and he began to move backward. Eventually, he had enough. Still screaming threats at me, he backed off, and I still followed him, throwing punches until finally, he turned and quickly retreated.

Many years later, in my sixties, I bumped into Dawn at a funeral. Despite the sad occasion, it was so nice to see her (and her Mother). We immediately chatted away as if we had seen each other every day during the fifty-odd intervening years. Amazingly, I felt that the bond remained between Dawn and I.

There were fifty prefabs in Banky Meadow and about fifty semi-detached brick houses up Woodland Avenue. Most of these housed families with children, some with several children. A total of some seventy-odd kids, ranging in age from toddlers to sixteen years or so, lived in the vicinity. Sixty-seven years later, as I sit writing this, I have just written down nearly all of their names, along with most of the names of their cats and dogs and some of their parents too. If only I could remember where I put my car keys and what I had for lunch last Sunday. Oh well, that's the age for you.

Jean and Jim

Our neighbours on the other side of Dawn and her Mum and Dad were particular friends of my Mum and Dad. Jean and Jim were really good neighbours, and I became firm friends with their two sons, Ian and Paul, especially Ian, who was about a year younger than me. My Dad and Jim went fishing together, and when we became old enough and learned how to swim, they took Ian and me with them. Ian and I joined cubs together and went swimming together and were good pals. Sometimes we would have a day out. Two families all together, and I can remember a few holidays, all of us together too.

They had a huge black dog which they imaginatively named Jet. As Jet grew up, he began to escape by leaping the three-foot high fence at the bottom of their garden into the cornfield beyond. If we were in the field and saw him coming, we would run away, but he easily caught up with us and would put his head down and head butt the back of a knee and bring us down one by one. One weekend Jim set to work on making the fence high enough to keep Jet in. He had obtained some six-foot lengths of corrugated iron from somewhere. These were fixed to the existing fence. Jim worked hard all day long on Saturday and well into Sunday. He planned to give them a good coat of paint the following weekend. He was just putting his tools back in the shed and telling my Dad, "That'll stop him from escaping," when someone let Jet out of the house. He ran down the garden and sailed over Jim's rebuilt fence and into the cornfield. Uncle Jim was livid. He was growling himself and swearing and threatening what he would do when he got hold of the "bloody daft mutt." However, that wasn't so easy. Now that he had raised the height of the fence to six-foot, he couldn't get over himself to fetch the dog back. He had to walk all the way around to get to the field and all the way back again. We were all in hysterics, but for once, Jim, who usually liked a laugh, didn't share in our merriment. However, in time he saw the funny side and roared with laughter whenever it came up in the conversation again.

Visitors

Visitors to our prefab were plentiful. Gran Wright would visit weekly. Her sister, my Aunt Sally, lived in Burbage at that time and would pop in from time to time and was sometimes invited for a meal with us. Mum's sister, my Auntie Mavis, visited regularly and played games with me and took me out for walks, and later on, as I grew older, we would go on bike rides together. Mum's younger sister Anne and brother Gordon visited fairly often, and they were always friendly and looked after me. My Nanna and Grandad Perkins (Lil and Walt) would catch a bus from Earl Shilton to Hinckley, then another to Burbage. The bus dropped them on Sapcote Road, and they would stroll through the jitty to Banky Meadow, often just in time for Sunday tea. Dad's sister, my Aunt Val, would visit and also spend a lot of time at Gran Wright's house with Mavis and Anne. Dad's Aunt Edna (Lil's sister) and Uncle Harry would join us for tea occasionally. Dad's cousins who lived at Rothley would somehow make their way to Hinckley and sleep

over every now and then. They were Brenda, Marlene and Avril. Little brother Chris was too young to come, so he stayed with his Mum, Nance (Gran Lil's sister), and his Dad, George, who we saw only once in a while.
My Uncle Ron, back home, de-mobbed from Army service in Egypt, had met a lady. She was a redhead from Newport, South Wales. Her name was Mavis, but Ron called her Ginge, and so we did too, mainly to save confusion with Mum's sister, also named Mavis. Ginge came to stay with us for quite a long spell. I liked her. She soon became my Auntie Ginge. They moved down to Newport in South Wales and married. Ginge had a son, Tony, from a previous relationship which we knew little about and, it being none of our business, never asked. They later had a son together when Andrew was born in 1958. I have always been proud of my Welsh cousins and always got on well with them, including, later, their wives. In due course, they would both have families of their own. They are really nice people with whom we still exchange odd letters or cards and even get together from time to time.

Once in a while, Ron would board a Black and White coach or a train and travel up from South Wales to visit us for a weekend. Sometimes he would bring a young but growing Andrew and occasionally Ginge and Tony too. Once in a while, we would travel down to Newport in my Dad's car to see them just for a day out. Sometimes we took other members of the family with us.

Characters

- CHARLIE

Charlie was a Character. Back then, in my Boyhood, I used to think he was a tramp. He certainly looked like one, and I wasn't aware of any fixed abode in connection with him. Looking back now, I really do wonder if he was a tramp, then why did he stay local? Anyway, he was a short scruffy fellow with a bristling beard. He always seemed to wear a huge overcoat and a flat cap, even indoors. He would visit certain pubs in Burbage and Hinckley on the scrounge. Always asking for a free beer on the house or asking a customer to buy him one or lend him money. I used to bump into him in all sorts of places like park benches, bus shelters and in the churchyard. One day I popped into the Burbage Reccy toilets for a wee, and there he was, sitting on the only toilet, fast asleep with the door wide open.

- OLD WALT

Another character remembered from my Burbage boyhood was known as 'Old Walt' I'm not sure that I ever knew his surname. Old Walt kept chickens. Quite a lot of them, in several locations. One of his hen houses was next to a cornfield which I always thought belonged to a local farmer. Years later, I learned that Old Walt owned it and another not far away. They were worth thousands of pounds. Despite this, Old Walt lived in an even older green bus. It was so old it had a permanent starting handle still hanging down in front of the radiator. However, it was hand-painted and waterproof. Most of the seats had been stripped out, and there was a proper bed pushed up to the back window. There was a stove and a sink inside too. Old Walt kept it clean and tidy. It was located on waste ground known to us kids as the sand 'ole, where we played a lot. In the summer, we would often knock on the bus door and ask Old Walt politely if we could have a drink of water. He would always welcome us and dip a cup into a big drum of fresh water. We had to share one cup, but he would refill it once or twice if necessary. He would chat away happily to us and seemed glad of a bit of company. We all agreed that he was an intelligent man and wondered why he lived on a bus. I still wonder. He must have been worth thousands.

- JACKIE

There was a little fellow who lived, up towards the top of Woodland Avenue, I think, with his Mother. His name was Jackie. He always seemed to wear a gaberdine raincoat. The belt was always pulled tight around his waist. He always wore a collar and tie and a huge flat cap. Jackie was always smartly dressed. He would always wander, alone, up and down the hill. Never straying very far from the house where he lived and never crossing the road. This poor soul had some sort of mental illness. He couldn't even talk. Instead, he would make 'talking noises' in the form of his own gibberish language but delivered in proper speech patterns with varied pitch and loudness, copied, I think, from his Mother. Most people gave him a wide berth, but I would stop for a few minutes and say hello to him. His face would break into a wide beam of pleasure. As he sort of got to know me, as soon as he recognized me approaching, his features would break into a huge grin, and he would greet me with obvious pleasure. He would keep shaking my hand and spouting his unintelligible gabble, and I would smile back at him and say the first thing that came to my head, and he would, in his own way, answer me, never losing eye-contact. I never stopped with Jackie for more than a few minutes, but I liked to think that he saw me as his friend and that I had, through our bizarre 'conversations' made his difficult life a little better, even if it was just for a few moments.

- THE FARMER

The Farmer could run fast for an old 'un. All of us kids agreed on that. When we trespassed on his land we never did any real harm. We might play football on his grass, climb up a tree, steal a bucket full of frogspawn, catch newts [which we always put back alive] or pick a few blackberries from his brambles. We may have pinched the odd apple, but nothing more serious or malicious. Once in a while, he would creep down towards us, hidden by a hedge, get as close as he could then surprise us by giving chase. He came very close a time or two but only caught me once. He didn't hurt me at all but held on to me firmly by the coat collar. Once he got his breath back, he informed me that if I did not appear at the farmhouse by the end of the day with a note from my Dad with my name and address on it, he would call the police. I had to go home and 'fess up' to my Dad. My mum went a bit hysterical, shouting at me because I had bought shame on the family. My Dad told her not to go over the top and that I hadn't done anything that he himself had not already done when he was a boy. My Dad told me not to pinch the Farmer's apples again and instructed me to tell The Farmer that my ear had been clipped by my Dad. [It wasn't on this occasion] I took the note up to the farmhouse and knocked on the door. The Farmer himself opened the door. I handed the note to him, and he read it and then, to my surprise, actually smiled at me. He asked me what my Dad had said about the incident, and I replied that Dad had clipped my earhole [even though he hadn't]. At that, he broke into a huge grin and courteously showed me out.

- PETER

When I was about ten years old, there was a local milkman who had his own Milk round, including Banky Meadow. Unlike the co-op which, when they first began calling locally, had a horse-drawn flatbed cart for milk delivery and a box cart for bread delivery, Peter Robinson had a smart new blue and white Bedford Milk Float. It had his name properly sign-written on both sides. He was a really nice chap, and one day, as he was delivering milk down our way, I asked him politely if I might be allowed to help him. He was a bit doubtful at first but gave me a spare hand crate from the van. Number 18 wants three silver tops, he said and nodded at the stacked crates on his float. I picked out three bottles [glass in those days], put them in the hand crate and delivered them to number 18. Following Peter's instructions, I collected two empty bottles and returned them to the 'empties crate' on the float.

As time passed, I began to help him more and more in our locality. As I got used to it and gained Peter's trust, I was able to focus on his instructions and remember four or five-door numbers at a time, along with their requirements. Peter arrived at Woodland Avenue at about 9.30 am, and on weekends and holidays when I was free to help him, irrespective of the weather, I would walk to the top of the Avenue at about 9.15 am and sit on the ground with my back to the wall to wait for his arrival. I would help him deliver in Woodland

Avenue and Banky Meadow, and within about three-quarters of an hour, he was gone to deliver all over Burbage, leaving me to play for the rest of the day.

I wasn't paid a wage or anything. I did it because I liked Peter and because I enjoyed it. However, I was well chuffed when, occasionally, he would reach into his leather cash satchel and flip me a florin [2 Shillings] or sometimes a half-crown [2 shillings and sixpence], which I always caught in mid-air and thanked him. I am fairly sure he appreciated my reliability and found me to be helpful. This carried on for just over a year until one day. He explained that I would be redundant now as he had gained a serious girlfriend who was going to help him on his rounds. I was quite sad and upset and moped around at home until I could get my head around my first rejection. Peter wished me well and gave me Five Bob [5 Shillings]. He always stopped for a moment to have a chat with me whenever we bumped into each other. He would always send my parents his regards and ask what I had been up to.

Burbage Co-op Bread Delivery 1950s

- FRANK

In the late 1950s, some seven or eight years after losing her husband, my Gran, Gladys Wright, met another man. At this time, all her children except for her youngest son Gordon had flown the nest. She still lived in the old corner terraced house in Hinckley. Left on her own, aged around 47 and had raised a family of five, she was at the stage when she had a little more free-time to herself. At weekends she enjoyed a drink with friends or her sister Sarah. One weekend she met Frank, who was just a few years older than her and struck up a friendship with him. They drank in moderation and talked together. If they could find a quiet corner in a club or pub, they would sit and hold hands like a couple of teenagers. They would visit different venues each weekend, but their favourites were the old Regent Club, the Railway Inn and the Castle Tavern. When it was time for Frank to catch the bus back to Burbage, where he lived with his two elder, unmarried sisters, they would withdraw into an entry or shop doorway, and Frank would take her in his arms and kiss her full on the lips. Just the once mind. I remember him being invited to family get-togethers, birthdays and the like, and he always chatted with me and often gave me money for a treat. However, what I have described here is the extent of their relationship. They never went on holiday together. She never stayed at his house, and he never stayed at hers. Theirs was just a deep fondness and respect for each other based mainly, I think, on companionship. Frank was a really smart fellow if a little old fashioned, his clothes were always really good quality. He always wore a hat, usually a Fedora. We never ever saw him without a shirt and tie and always a suit with razor-sharp creases in the trousers. Always had a silk handkerchief in his jacket top pocket and highly polished real leather shoes. A real Gentleman, he raised his hat when greeting people and held doors open for Gladys [he treated her like a queen]. He would stand if anyone came into a room and always walked next to the curb with Gladys on the inside. Frank epitomized the old-school gentleman in every way.

- Children

There were fifty prefabs in Banky Meadow and about fifty semidetached brick houses up Woodland Avenue. Most of these housed families with children, some with several children. A total of some seventy-odd kids, ranging in age from toddlers to sixteen years or so, lived in the vicinity. Sixty-seven years later, as I sit writing this, I have just written down nearly all of their names, along with most of the names of their cats and dogs and some of their parents too. If only I could remember where I put my car keys and what I had for lunch last Sunday. Oh well, that's the age for you.

At any one time, there could be about 20 or 30 of us playing together. The older ones looked after the younger ones and protected them from any serious risk. Not just siblings but any younger child. Nobody asked them to do this. They just did it. The older kids would often organize a game to include the whole range of ages present at that time. Thus, there were parades and medieval battles with toy plastic swords or homemade ones made from wood. Another day we would all become cowboys and cowgirls, another day, we would re-enact battles from World War Two, or we would be spacemen and aliens from outer space. A part-built double garage on the edge of the sand-hole became, in turn, a cinema, a pub, a hotel, a submarine, a wild west saloon, or a theatre. Our imagination knew no limits.

CHAPTER THREE: INFANT SCHOOL

Each Christmas, we put on the traditional; nativity play. Being a shy boy, I did not want to be picked for a part, and my luck held out each year I was at St. Catherine's, and I was never selected. I did, however, enjoy the carol singing. For the first two years at school, Santa would visit us, and each of us was called out, in turn, to receive a Christmas present from Santa. My first present was a box with a game in it. The game was tiddlywinks. My second present was a box with a game in it. Tiddlywinks again. I remember drafting a letter to Santa. I cannot remember the exact words, but it was along the lines of "Get a grip Santa, what the bloody hell do I need all these tiddly-winks for....any chance of a new bike instead?" I never sent it, and to be honest now, well, I'm glad I didn't.

Mum Prepares For My Education

In 1956 a huge event in my life took place. I started school. Once again, Mum had planned well in advance and saved each week for months on end so that when the time came, I had some serviceable decent clothes to wear. In those days, boys had to wear shorts for school until they went to high school aged eleven. A gabardine raincoat, gloves, a woollen balaclava [which she had knitted herself] for cold days, and a soft faux leather helmet for rainy days. Both of these were very popular back in those days. The list was not as long as modern-day school requirements but included a string-drawn "pump bag" containing plimsolls. These were not available in Francis's, Harold Wightman, or any other shop. They were made by everyone's Mum using any scrap material or off-cut of a fairly robust nature. Sewn up into a sort of envelope and closed at the neck by a draw string which was left quite long to form a handle with which to carry it. Mine was navy blue and white gingham checked.

First Day

It was a fifteen-minute walk to Burbage Saint Catherine's Church of England School. With only one quiet road to cross close to home. My Dad came home from working a night shift, and since Mum had to go to Hinckley to work, instead of going straight to bed, he walked me to school first. [We had no car at this stage] I felt so embarrassed because I felt it was entirely unnecessary for him to do this. It made me feel stupid. I knew the way and couldn't understand the need for this. I asked Dad not to meet me at midday, as had been previously mentioned. When we arrived at the school, Dad asked me if I wanted him to take me inside. I told him firmly that I was okay. "Dad, honestly, go home, get some sleep." My feelings outweighed my natural shyness, but as I walked through the school door for the first time, I really did shake with nerves.

I was asked my name and directed to the correct classroom. As I walked into the classroom, the teacher told me off for playing on the coke pile in the corner of the playground. I was off on the wrong foot. I felt that the telling-off was unfair. I hadn't yet been told what the school rules were, and since there was no warning sign near the coke pile, how was I supposed to know it was out of bounds? However, my fear gradually subsided throughout the day as I found my way around, talked to some of the other pupils and came to understand that the teacher was there to be obeyed but certainly wasn't an ogre. We did some drawing for quite a while leading up to mid-morning playtime. Mum had made me a small cheese sandwich wrapped in greaseproof paper [no Tupperware in those days]. At morning playtime, I retrieved this from my pump bag hanging in the cloakroom and munched it with the free-issue third of a pint of milk. This was called lunch, and no doubt in Mum's mind prevented me from wasting away. In those days, we always called our main meal of the day 'dinner' regardless of whether we ate it at noon or in the evening. After wolfing down my lunch, I still had about ten minutes left to have a quick wee. The toilets were in a separate building, and to be honest, it was a good job they were. They stunk to high heaven. There was no roof over the boy's urinal, so it could be quite cold and wet going for a wee against the black wall. Competitions held amongst the boys to see who could wee the highest didn't help matters.

St Catherine's Church School, Burbage

I would then have a while to run around the playground to exercise my legs and lungs. It's a well-known fact that small boys are incapable of running without also whooping, screaming or shouting. The duty teacher rang a hand bell to tell us that playtime was over, and we lined up in our classes and filed silently into the school. On that first day, I remember playing with a small spade, a jam jar and a huge box of sand. All too soon, it was 'dinner' time. I then had one hour to walk home, eat my dinner and walk back to school again.

Depending on what shift Dad was on, he would usually warm through a dinner prepared by Mum the evening before. Alternatively, Mum would catch a bus home from Hinckley or sometimes even walk home from her job in a hosiery factory in Upper Castle Street to see to it that I had a hot dinner. Why on earth my parents put themselves under such pressure is beyond me. Surely it would have been better to have a snack at 12.30 and have our main meal in the evening. This is, in fact, what we ended up doing, but it was quite a while later.

On this first day at school and often thereafter, I used to get into trouble for 'dawdling' and for frustrating my parents, who rushed around like whirling dervishes getting me a dinner to eat and getting me back to school and themselves back to work in time for our respective afternoon stints, whilst I took ages to get home because I had been dawdling or zig-zagging home playing at cowboys or something instead of walking directly home.

Upon return to school on this first day, we had a very pleasant afternoon. A screen was drawn back, and the neighbouring teacher (who played piano) and her class joined us in a sing-song. I enjoyed learning the tunes and words to such songs as Soldier, Soldier, Won't You Marry Me? Bobby Shafto and Michael Finnegan (Begin Again), after which the other class disappeared as the screen was drawn again, and our own teacher read us a story from the Noddy series of books by Enid Blyton.

Lunchtime

After a few weeks at school, a boy in my class whose Mum never packed him a mid-morning lunch asked the teacher if he could go to the toilet. This happened every day. It was always near to and before mid-morning playtime. You'd have thought the teacher would have cottoned on. He would then go to the cloakroom where all the pump bags hung and steal the lunch made for me by my Mum and quickly scoff it down before returning to class. I knew it was him, but we were not allowed food in class, and my shy and timid nature meant that I was too scared to tackle him. I was, in fact, bullied by him and a few other boys too. This continued on and off when I went up to Junior School and also into my first year at High School. It took all that time for me to see red and explode again like I had done when Dawn was pushed over by the bully back in those pre-school years.

Playtime and Games

Unless we had really bad weather, it was compulsory to spend our playtimes outside in the playground. There was a huge pile of coke for the school heating system boiler in one corner. The toilets for girls and boys were in another corner. A climbing frame stood in the third corner, and a storage shed for PE equipment etc., in the fourth. There was also a tall frame or gantry, which must at one-time support swings or something similar. This was used by the boys for shinning up.

This left a sizeable clear space for us boys to play at being planes (with arms outstretched for wings), trains (with arms, left and right alternatively pumping backward and forwards like pistons), cars (with hands steering our movements with an imaginary steering wheel) or a cowboy holding imaginary reins in front. In each case, the appropriate sounds had to be made, which made for a very loud cacophony to which the girls added chanted rhymes for skipping or shouted numbers from those playing hopscotch.

During games lessons, the storage shed was unlocked by the teacher and footballs, wooden hoops etc., were utilised for organized team games. Coloured cotton bands were worn over one shoulder to denote that you were in the blue team or green or yellow, or red.

After School

I dawdled home, retrieved the door key from our hiding place and let myself in to find a light tea waiting for me on the kitchen table, typically a banana and a couple of ginger biscuits. This would suffice until Mum came home from work. Once these were scoffed and washed down with milk, I would hang up my school clothes, change into old play clothes and go outdoors and play for a while. If my Dad was on nights, my Auntie Mavis would turn up for supper and stay the night as Mum was of a very nervous disposition. More often than not, the three of us would share a pan of home-made chips for supper, sometimes with a slice of bread spread thinly with margarine to make a chip butty.

My First School Trip

After a year, I moved up to year two, where I remember doing well in English and particularly well with my reading but not doing well at much else. I remember only one school trip, and we went to Kenilworth Castle and then on to Warwick Castle. I remember not one but three highlights from this momentous educational trip. One was the bus ride itself. My lifelong love of vehicles had already begun, and I loved the unmistakable, distinctive engine sound of the Bedford OM series bus. I can recognize the sound of this engine a mile away even now I'm in my seventies.

The second highlight was the dinner-time discovery that, along with the sandwiches, crisps, wafers and apples packed for me by Mum, she had also included a surprise small bottle of Lime juice which I loved but, due to the cost, did not often receive. The third highlight, and best of all, came when the bus driver fell down the steps at the bus door and landed unceremoniously on his backside in the car park. Children can be cruel. We all laughed ourselves silly until, having got his breath back and rubbed his backside a bit, he pulled himself back up the steps into the bus and glared angrily at us for a full minute. The laughter abruptly subsided. I think the school's educational slant on the trip was wasted on me. I was not in the slightest bit interested in castles and history, and this would remain the case until I retired and found an interest in history after researching my family history late on in life.

The Generous Farmer

Another treat I remember from school was when a local farmer bought in a live lamb for the children, each in turn to stroke and pet. Another time he bought in his sheepdog for us all to pet, and yet another time, an old zinc bath lined with newspaper and containing apples for us kids, picked fresh from his orchard that morning. An orderly queue was formed, and one by one, we helped ourselves to an apple from the old zinc bath. My mate David Bottomley, from his position behind me in the queue, whispered hoarsely in my ear, "Pick a big bugger, Den" I ignored him and picked the apple nearest to me as my turn came. I got back to my desk and turned to Dave, but I couldn't see his face. His head was obscured from view by the biggest apple I had ever seen before or since. Dave still managed to polish off his apple before I was halfway through mine. What strange things stick in our minds [For over 65 years in this case].

The Headmistress Listens To Me Reading

One day the headmistress, Miss Wheelock, entered our classroom. The hubbub within the class room subsided as about 40 children felt suddenly unsettled and a little anxious. We only ever saw Miss Wheelock at assembly when morning prayers were the order of the day or when someone was in trouble. Her appearance scared us all a bit as we each wondered who was in trouble. It turned out that no-one was. One by one, each of us had to follow her into the nearby corridor, where she sat on a chair and listened to us reading to her aloud from the current class reading book. When it was my turn, I read about five pages before she said, "OK, Dennis, that will do. What a good reader you are. Excellent! Well done."

I honestly had no idea before that moment that I was a good reader. No one had ever told me before. I liked my teacher, but she wasn't too good at praising pupils. Come to think of it. She wasn't too good at motivating us at all.

The Grove Road Hut

Things changed slightly in my final year at St. Catherine's. The school was overcrowded in those days, so they hired the hut located just around the corner on Grove Road. It belonged to the nearby Conservative Club. It was huge with a kitchen, toilets, a stage and side rooms. It was used for village shows, boy scout pantomimes etc and could be hired for weddings etc., but it was my classroom for my final year at St. Catherine's Church Infant School. There was a huge aviary next door where the local butcher kept peacocks and peahens as a hobby. These made a lot of noise at times, but they never bothered us.

The Grove Road Conservative Hut. Seen here near the end of its life, shortly before demolition. Back then, it was kept in really good condition.

Looking back, as my time at Saint Catherine's Infant School approached an end, the teachers had done their job. I could do simple addition, subtraction, multiplication and division sums. I knew that there were sixty seconds in a minute, sixty minutes in an hour, twenty-four hours in a day, seven days in a week, fifty-two weeks or three hundred and sixty-five days, or twelve calendar months in a year. I could name the days of the week and months of the year in order. I had learned in that pre-metric age that there were twelve inches in a foot, three feet in a yard, two pints in a quart and 8 pints in a gallon. Furthermore, I knew that there were sixteen ounces in a pound, fourteen pounds in a stone and many more basic learning requirements.

All of this meant that English school kids were of much superior intelligence to our continental counterparts, who only had to be able to understand TENS of everything to facilitate the metric system. Huh, that was too simple for clever clogs like us. We broke up for the long summer holidays feeling confident and looking forward to 'going up' to Junior school. My first school, St Catherines Church School, is sadly no longer there. It was demolished to make way for housing.

Our First Car

Not long after I started school, my Dad bought a second-hand 1939 Ford 10 from a chap he knew who lived near my Grandparents in Earl Shilton. In those days, it was customary to give your car a name, and we called ours Ada. I was so chuffed, especially since Mum preferred to sit in the back seats, and I was allowed to sit in the front. There was no heater and no screen washers. Ada did have a defroster bar. This was a bar about 300mm long, which was stuck to the inside of the screen, near the bottom, behind the driver's wheel, with a rubber sucker on each end. The bar contained a thin wire coil which was then connected to the car battery via the bulkhead. It incorporated a simple toggle switch, and when switched on, the coil heated up and cleared a small patch of the windscreen of mist or, eventually, ice for the driver to peer through rather like peering through a letterbox. There was no automatic choke. Instead of flashing indicators, it had small orange arms called trafficators, which flick up, left or right, to warn other drivers that a left-hand or right-hand turn was about to be negotiated. Some of them lit up. Drivers had to carry out more arm-signals through the driver's open window in those days. It was seventeen years old, very basic, black and a bit battered, but we loved it. There were only about three cars in our neighbourhood of about a hundred houses at that time. One day when Mum wasn't with us, Dad had Ada up to 50 miles per hour, and I really thought we would take off.

My Dad's First Car – A 1939 Ford 10.

CHAPTER FOUR: SUNDAY SCHOOL

When I was a boy, Sundays were totally different from what they are today. Nobody indulged in much activity, particularly if it was a noisy one. For religious people, it was a day of worship, but more generally, it was a day of quiet rest. Few shops opened on a Sunday in those days. When I was six, I was sent to Sunday School. Every Sunday afternoon, an elderly and kindly gentleman would call for my mate from next door and me. The three of us would walk up into Burbage Village to the Congregational Chapel. His name was Mr. Hood. After Sunday School, Mr. Hood would then make sure we got home safely.

The Infant Section

Burbage Congregational Sunday School from 1956 to 1963 was a happy place. My first Sunday school teacher in the infant section was Betty, and she welcomed me and made sure I knew where to hang my coat and where the toilet was, and so on. We sang songs and hymns, which I soon got to know, and I always enjoyed singing along. We were also told stories that either related directly to Jesus or had a moral theme written into the story. We also got involved in various activities, such as making our parents' various items such as Calendars, Christmas cards, Easter cards and small floral arrangements for Mother's Day, etc. Betty was assisted by a beautiful young lady called Wendy. Now I really liked Betty, but I instantly fell in love with Wendy even at that tender age.

Burbage Congregational Chapel To The Left Of The Row Of Cottages

Playmates

We were issued with a glossy, coloured, illustrated religious pamphlet especially written for small children to take home. It was called Playmate and was all about the theme chosen for the lesson, prayer and discussion on that particular Sunday. Two collections were taken. One at the beginning of proceedings was to pay for your playmate. Then about halfway through, a box with a coin slot in the top was passed around. We were required to put an old pre-decimal penny in each one. The second one was for Jesus, and we all had to sing a little ditty over and over until everyone had put their penny in the box.

Dropping, dropping, dropping, dropping

Hear the pennies fall

Every one, for Jesus

He shall have them all

At that young and tender age and not being very bright, I used to wonder what there was in heaven that cost so much that Jesus needed all that money. Was there a one-armed bandit or something? I wondered.

The Junior Section

After a couple of years, we left the infant section and entered the junior section. This was run along very similar lines but more in line with our age as we grew older. There were a few differences, though. We always kicked things off with communal prayers and a hymn. This was usually led by George Lea. George was a funny man and always made us laugh, but there was always a religious or moral point to his little talk. In later years George became Pastor of the Chapel.

After that, we would split up into groups of about six children according to our age, and each group would have the same Sunday School Teacher every week for a half-hour discussion covering many topics. We were allowed to call our teachers by their first names. They were all really nice people and made you feel at ease. Even shy kids like me became comfortable and were encouraged to contribute to the discussion. So it was that I enjoyed learning about all sorts of things from the Sunday School Teachers. After the group discussions, we all joined together again for a final hymn, prayer and notices.

Our Pastor

Occasionally our Pastor would drop in to see us, usually with a message or a notice of some sort. He preached to the public during the services held in the main church each Sunday Morning and Evening. Such was our respect for him that we didn't even know his first name. Everyone, children, teachers and the general congregation, always addressed him formally as Mr. Thompson. He was quite high up in the Government Probation Service.

The Sunday School Treats

Each July, all the local Sunday Schools joined together for what we called the Sunday School Treats. First of all, a huge parade took place with banners, flags and brass bands marching around the streets of Hinckley, interspersed with flatbed lorries done up in religious themes and gathering 'en-masse' in the Borough. Throngs of worshipping marchers, singing and praying together. After this, all the children, Sunday School Teachers and helpers would return to their respective churches and chapels for a huge tea laid on by volunteers from the Sunday School. Sandwiches, home-made cakes, jam tarts and biscuits followed by trifle, fruit and cream, all washed down with orange squash. It was wonderful.

After this, we would rest a while to allow some digestion, then play a few quiet games. After that, we would walk through the jitty from the Horse Pool to the Grove Road Junior School, which always gave us permission to use their playing field and some sports equipment. Our Sunday school teachers would then organize egg and spoon races, sack races, three-legged races, and wheelbarrow races, and the older children would compete in the 100 yards sprint, high jump and long jump. A drinking fountain in the school playground ensured that we all remained hydrated. It would be about six 'o' clock in the evening by the time we had put the equipment away and walked back to our chapel. It doesn't sound much by today's standards, but to us, it was a great day that we all looked forward to with excitement. We would talk non-stop to our parents that evening about the day's events and go to bed very tired but very content. Life was all so simple then it seemed.

Sunday School Treats Walk c1960

Sunday School Treats me on a float as Joseph. It took me ages to grow the beard.

The Annual Sermons

We also looked forward to our annual anniversary sermons held in September. For a month before sermons day, instead of our normal Sunday school activities, after one prayer and a short lesson, we filed into the main church for choir practice, where we practiced and practiced four hymns under the guidance of a qualified choirmaster. This was serious stuff. We knew that come to Sermons Day. The church would be absolutely full of parents and the general congregation. We had to get this right and put on a good show for them. We only had four practices. The choirmaster did not mess about. He made us work hard until we could sing the hymns how he wanted us to sing them.

When the day came, we all wore our best clothes. In fact, most children had brand-new clothes for the occasion. This was hard on some families who were struggling with little spare money, my parents included. My Mum planned well in advance and paid a small amount weekly into a co-op scheme. The money would be redeemed at the co-op store a couple of weeks before the big day to set me up with new shoes or sandals, socks, trousers, shirt, tie or dickie bow, and jacket.

Scrubbed up and with a recent "Jack Veasey special haircut" [more of this later], we entered the church and climbed up the steep stairs to the high choir stalls and waited in quiet but excited anticipation of the arrival of parents. Mr. Thompson began the service and then introduced the first hymn. At last, we were away, and we sang our hearts out. I have always enjoyed music and singing, and I really enjoyed myself. The joy for me was the knowledge that we were singing the hymns exactly as they should be, thanks to practicing with a proper choirmaster.

Scrubbed up well for the sermons

Prize Giving Sunday

Another event was prize-giving Sunday. Your prize was mainly based on your attendance. There were points to be gained from every service attended. This put me at a disadvantage because quite a lot of kids with church-going parents attended morning service with their parents, Sunday School in the afternoon, and evening service with their parents, whereas I only attended afternoon Sunday school unless it was a special occasion. The result was that I only won "Consolation" prizes. All the prizes were Christian books. However, I always won a nice enough book each year, and what is more, I still have all eight of them in my collection. This sparked off a lifelong appreciation of books and reading, and as I write this, I am surrounded by hundreds of books on all sorts of topics

My first [of Eight] prize books from Sunday School.

John Williams - Missionary

In 1962 (aged 11), I did win a special prize. We had been having discussions at Sunday school about Missionaries and their work. We were given a smallish cardboard flat pack assembled into a money box about the size of a two- pound bag of sugar (or 1 kilo). We were asked to raise as much money as we could to send to fund the John Williams missionary ship. By doing odd jobs etc., I managed to raise the sum of nine shillings, a fair effort for an eleven-year-old at the time. The approximate equivalent value, as I write today, is £10.00

Dennis Perkins collected £ 9 s. - d.
for the ships of the London Missionary Society

Essay Competition

However, I did not win my special prize for collecting nine shillings. The Sunday school teachers organized a trip for those who were interested. A coach load of us went to London to see the John Williams Missionary Ship moored on the Thames. Afterward, we were treated to fish and chips in a Thames-side restaurant, then visited Madame Tussaud's waxworks before returning home tired but content after an interesting and entertaining day.

We were invited to enter a competition. The best essay about John Williams, the missionary, his ships, his work and the day trip would win a prize. Now I am slow with numbers (I usually get there in the end), but I have always loved reading and writing, so I entered my essay. Seventeen entries were whittled down to two, but the judges could not separate them. It was eventually decided to award two prizes. I still have mine. It was another book, but it did not say "Consolation Prize" on the inscription. It says;

Burbage Congregational Sunday School

Presented to Dennis Perkins for his essay on "John Williams VII" London Trip 1962

It may not seem much, but I have always been proud of my first recognised achievement. Unfortunately, I don't remember what became of the written essay.

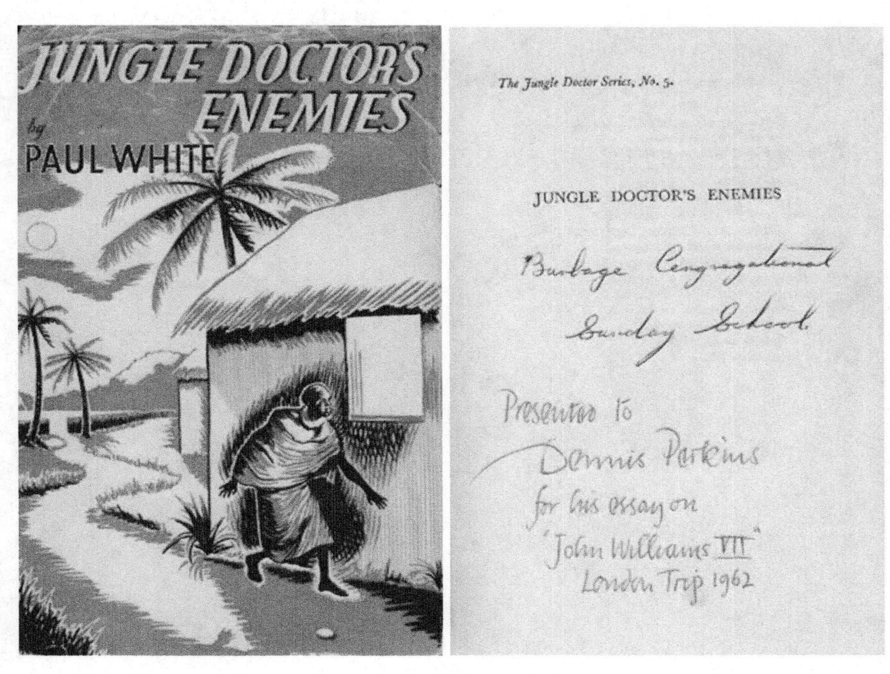

The Parting of the Ways

The following year I began to drift away from the "Burbage Congs" I continued to attend their Youth Club for a while, where we played games, especially table tennis, drank tea or orange squash, and sometimes did physical activities such as a run round the village and occasionally put on our own shows. It didn't go down too well with the teachers that some of us were taking advantage of the Youth club facilities but no longer putting in proper attendance at Sunday school. In addition, I was becoming interested in girls and also began to find other activities to involve myself in, like fishing and football. I was also given a 'talking-to' when I was caught smoking in the Sunday school yard. Even then, I knew that it was a fair enough telling-off, and I didn't want to generate any further ill feelings to spoil what previously had been a happy relationship lasting for eight years. So, without losing my affection and total respect for the place and the people, I quietly drifted away.

CHAPTER FIVE: WHAT WE GOT UP TO

As each of us grew older and learned more sense, often by mistakes and misadventures, we, in turn, looked out for the younger ones. For example, one of my "mistakes" was to drop a penny banger firework into a wasp nest. I got stung on my eyelid for my troubles. It swelled right up, closed my eye and caused me much pain. A few years later, I saw a younger playmate light a penny banger and shove it inside a horizontal scaffold tube at head height. It made for an even louder bang, but if you pushed it too deep into the tube or pushed it into the tube too soon before the banger had properly started to fizz, it would often be starved of oxygen and fizzle out. The young fellow then put his eye to the end of the tube to check it was still alight. I whacked his ear so hard that his head jerked sideways just a split second before the firework went off. He howled and had a red ear for a while, but I reckon I almost certainly saved him from eye damage.

Fun and Games

The flow of traffic was light and slow-moving, so it was quite safe for us to play football and cricket at the T- junction near our house whilst the girls hopscotched, hula hooped, skipped and pushed dolls around in prams further along the street. A lamp post and a bush served as goalposts and a fire hydrant as a wicket. If we had more time, we could visit the recreation ground at the top of the Avenue. We called it the rec or reccy. There was a narrow lane leading from one corner, which came out in the Cross Keys pub yard.

One of our favourite pastimes was hurtling at great speed down the long hill that was Woodland Avenue leading on to Banky Meadow. We 'hurtled' down this hill on bikes, scooters, trolleys, roller skates and on one occasion, six of us on an old settee until the castors broke near the bottom of the hill and unceremoniously dumped all of us onto the road. As a result, the six of us had a wonderful array of scratches, grazes and bruises. My dog, a West Highland White Terrier, followed me everywhere and insisted on riding on the front of my trolley even when I was 'hurtling' down the hill. He loved it. His little ears would flap as we picked up speed on the way down, and he would actually lean into the left-hand bend at the bottom of the hill like a motorcyclist banking into a bend.

Behind me, you can see the long hill we used to "hurtle" down.

Me and faithful companion ready for a hurtle.

All the boys had a Dinky toy car collection which kept us entertained for hours. We would drag a flat hand or sometimes a small piece of wood along the gravel to make roads for our "Dinky cars" There were crazes, of course, playing with conkers, marbles, pea shooters, catapults, bubble gum cards which could be just saved up to form a collection or flicked against a wall in a game of skill. We would play for hours riding on our bikes, scooters, trolleys or roller skates. We would sometimes become our heroes from early TV programs and Saturday morning picture clubs. Bows and arrows would be fashioned from string, nicked from Dad's shed and suitable sticks cut from trees. A stout stick would become a Tommy-gun or rifle. So, one day we might be Robin Hood, and the next day, Zorro, the Scarlet Pimpernel, Davy Crocket, or cowboy Roy Rogers.

When I was on my own, it never bothered me at all. I was always content with my own company. I would occupy myself. For instance, I would often tip my trolley on its side and, sitting on the door step drive my 'lorry' or 'bus' for hours on end using the trolley's pram wheel as a steering wheel.

Scrumping

We wandered far and wide as free as birds and only went home when we were hungry and not always then. We would sometimes light a fire in a camp out in the fields, and roast potatoes scrounged or stolen, in the embers. Sometimes it would be apples following a raid on an orchard. Nearly all the boys carried a penknife, and a suitable stick would be cut from the hedge, sharpened like a large pencil into a point, and bark shaved off for about four inches from the point. An apple or spud would then be stuck on the end of the stick, pulled onto the shaved portion of the stick and held over the fire embers until cooked. Delicious!

Clay Raids

Occasionally a similar stick would be prepared, and we would head for the sand'ole for there were several small clay holes there, and by lying on the ground and pushing our arm into the hole, right up to the armpit, we could just reach and extract enough clay, to roll into several small balls, about the size of golf balls. Split into two teams. We would face "the enemy" some 30 or 40 yards away. The clay balls were our ammunition. One by one, we would stick them onto the pointed and shaved portion of our stick. The whip of the stick, when moved in a swatting action, had an amazing effect on the clay balls. When the stick stopped dead at the end of the "swat," the clay balls would fly off the end at a tremendous speed. Most of us became experts at judging speed, direction and trajectory. In other words, we became good shots. If you stopped one of these clay balls, it hurt like hell and usually resulted in a bruise the next day. I remember once a boy being knocked out cold for several seconds when a flying clay ball thundered into his temple. Luckily, he made a full recovery. Clay sticks weren't the only weapon we had in our arsenal. All manner of sticks and staffs along with home-made swords, bows and arrows, catapults and pea-shooters, squeezy bottles for water pistols, and when we could afford them, stink bombs and itching powder.

Al Fresco

In the summer, we kids would often go for a picnic over the fields or down Burbage Woods. Sometimes we would be gone all day. We would each carry a "duffle bag" containing our brown sauce sandwiches (we called it 'bren-sauce') and a small bottle of water. Our bag would also be utilised to carry any fruit we scrumped to supplement our sandwiches.

Barber Shop Visits

Periodically boys would be told, "You are not going out on Saturday morning. Your Dad is taking you to get your haircut." This was greeted with groans of protest. Most of the local lads hated going for a haircut. Having a haircut at Jack Veasey's barber shop opposite St Catherine's Church in Burbage was not an enjoyable experience. Jack was a nice enough man, well-liked and respected. The problem was that he liked to chat whilst at his work. I felt that his attention was never fully on his job, for he would trap a swathe of hair between his index and middle (big) finger to straighten it out, then cut a straight line close to his fingers in true barber style, BUT…just as he got to the end of the cut his hand would jerk away before the cut had quite completed. This had the effect of yanking a hair or two painfully out of their follicles at the very end of the scissor-cut. This was repeated on almost every cut. Us boys spent the entire time in nervous anticipation of the final painful tug. We could hardly breathe. If we could not contain ourselves and let out a squeak of agitation or pain, Jack would just carry on regardless, happily chatting away. An occasional louder yowl from a younger boy would be met with surprise from Jack, followed by short shrift. "Now then, sit still. What's up wi' yer?" but his bark was worse than his bite. Actually, he could be quite funny and despite it all, we liked and respected him.

Cinema

My first experience of going to the "pictures," as we called it, was when a few close friends and myself attended Saturday Morning picture Club at the Regent cinema. They were always well attended, and even though we would arrive early, we still had to join a large queue outside and wait noisily but patiently until Mr. Fray, the Manager, let us in, about thirty at a time. The usual order of events was "Coming to this Cinema soon" [which is self-explanatory] followed by "Look at Life," which was a ten-minute interesting look at some aspect of British Life. Then there would be a few miscellaneous cartoons followed by an intermission during which, If we were lucky, we might manage to buy an orange drink.

We would spend our bus-fare home on sweets or popcorn. Following this break, the main film began. Sometimes it would be a comedy such as Mr. Pastry, Norman Wisdom, or even Ukulele man George Formby. Others were action thriller movies like The Scarlet Pimpernel, Zorro, and Robin Hood. Cops and robbers films were always popular, and war films always went down well, but the favourite was a good old western during which all the kids would excitedly cheer the goodies [especially the cavalry] and boo or hiss at the baddies.

At the end of all this, a rowdy crowd of kids poured out into Lancaster Road. We now had to leg it all the way back to Burbage because we had blown our bus fare on sweets, but we had to get a move on so as not to be late for dinner. We would trot all the way home. The manner of the trot would depend on the film we had just watched. Our legs would obviously be doing the trotting, but our arms would be operating a steering wheel, [cops and robbers] or reigns of a horse [western], the pistons of a train [Casey Jones], the wings of a plane (war film) and so on. There were two other cinemas in town at that time. The best one was the Odeon in the Borough, and there was also the Danilo on the corner of Trinity Lane and Hollycroft.

Reading

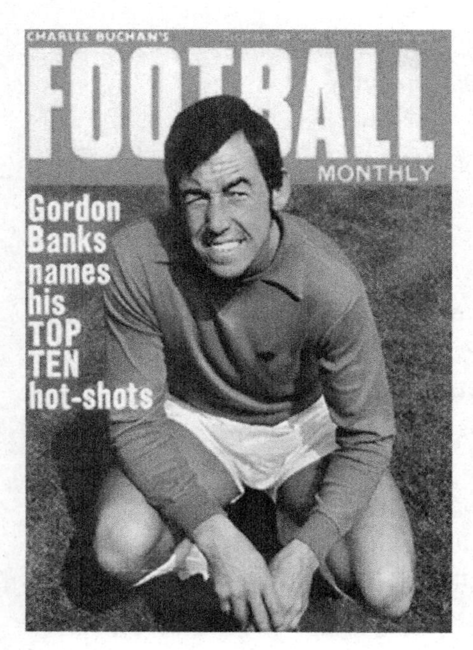

I was allowed two comics a week. I chose the Beezer and the Topper. My mate received the Beano and the Dandy, and once read, we would swap them. So I read at least four comics a week and really enjoyed them. The girls had their own comics, notably “Girl” and “Bunty.”

As we got a little bit older, we changed to action comics as opposed to purely humorous ones. The most popular of these was the Eagle, but personally, I preferred the Victor. Finally, a little older still, I changed to Football Monthly.

CHAPTER SIX: FUR, FEATHERS, AND FINS

If you are not interested in fishing, please do not be deterred from reading this chapter. It is more about the things that happened to me whilst fishing, often humorous and also about wildlife I have observed at close quarters because I was sitting still and quiet in the countryside.

I did a lot of fishing as a boy. For me, fishing is not just about catching fish. Yes, we want to, and yes, we try to, but it's not the be-all and end-all. Fishing should also incorporate the enjoyment of companionship, humour, being out and about, the fresh air, scenery, wildlife, and all that is happening around you in the countryside. I have tried to demonstrate this when writing this book. Those who purely focus on the biggest fish or heaviest net, or technical details, in my opinion, miss out on so much. However, each to his own. This is only my humble opinion.

The Many Joys of Fishing

It is not surprising that I became interested in fishing since I come from a run of at least four generations of coarse fishermen to my knowledge, and possibly more. An interest in coarse fishing for me brought with it not just a liking for being out in the fresh air but also an appreciation of the countryside and an intrigue for all creatures great and small who came a lot nearer to me because I was sitting still and quietly in their domain and so their colours, behaviour and charms became easier to observe and further attract me.

A Blackbird perches on my rod for a rest.

I am fortunate enough to have had close encounters with wild rabbits, brown hares, field mice, dragonflies, kingfishers, water voles, foxes, badgers, and all kinds of waterfowl. Herons and all kinds of birds whilst I was sitting still and quietly fishing.

Birds often perch on fishing rods as they lie still in the rod rests. When I was young, water voles were aplenty, and it was not unusual for fishermen to watch them bankside and in the water going about their daily search for food. They are such endearing little creatures. Indeed, fishermen in those days would often involuntarily start in surprise as they looked down to see a water vole washing itself, sitting close to them. The water vole would sometimes also start and look up at the fisherman and then carry on with ablutions. I have been privileged to quietly observe foxes, hares, deer, rabbits, rats, squirrels, field mice, dragonflies, damsel flies, kingfishers, great crested grebe and all sorts of insects and birds too numerous to list and most of them too clever to stay long enough to be photographed by a slow rumbling old plodder like me.

Four Generations of Anglers

My Grandad, Walter Perkins. 1901–1969 (No fancy tackle, but still caught loads of fish).

My Dad, aka Raymond Perkins. 1929 – 2010. Over 75 years' experience. Very wise.

Here's one he caught earlier (1954).

Me, Dennis Perkins 1950 – Living.

My Son, aka Kevin Raymond Perkins. 1977 – Living. Shows me how to do it again.

Early Encounters with All Creatures, Great and Small

My earliest fascination with all manner of creatures began at the tender age of two and a half years. I would sit in our back garden for hours on end, digging rigorously with my red-painted metal seaside spade with a wooden handle. Occasionally I would come across a worm. Wow, these were fun. Stretching them to enormous lengths, trying to pull them from the earth. Holding them and squeezing tight to feel them attempting to wriggle in my hand. Trying to tie them in a knot was also good fun and occasionally chopping one in half to watch the two halves wriggling. I loved worms. I was not old enough to realize my own cruelty.

In those early days of infancy, I had my own creature in the form of a huge grey cat named 'Fluff,' who we inherited from the previous incumbents of our council-rented prefab. I loved Fluff and longed to cuddle her. Unfortunately, she was not used to children and would not allow me even to get close to her. Determined to stroke her, one day, I cornered her and made a grab for her. She reacted with a yowl and clawed the back of my hand quite badly, and quickly hid beneath the sideboard. I was an unsteady, early toddler at the time, but my memory was clear. I took off the royal blue beret I was wearing, bent down, and made several swipes with it at the poor cat. Luckily I didn't connect. Again, I was just not old enough to understand. Not until Mum told me, in very clear terms, not to do it again. I didn't.

I was bought up in the 1950s in a rural area on the edge of Burbage, a Leicestershire Village. If I slipped through the gap in our hedge at the bottom of our garden, I would find myself on the edge of a large Cornfield. It was here that I first saw the grey horses pulling the plough and heard the whistles, clanging of chains, and shouts to the toiling, plodding horse from the plough handler. The birds flocked to follow the plough and take advantage of the rich pickings as the sliced soil was turned. The sight and sounds of that scene stayed with me in my head for the rest of my life. On the other side of the cornfield was the main road. Back in those days, it was considered a busy road, but by today's standards, it was fairly quiet. I wasn't allowed to cross that road until I was old enough to have "road sense," and I was deemed to have that at about the age of six (Things were different then).

I was really glad to reach this early milestone in life because it meant that, after crossing the main road, I was able to follow a track into a tree-lined field containing a huge pond. I went forth with my friend, Ian. We were armed with a fishnet on the end of a cane, which we had pestered our parents to buy for us for an old sixpence or a tanner each. (2½ new pence) We also took a large jam jar each, with a tied string handle. In a small bag, we both had sustenance in the form of "brensauce," which is what we called bread with margarine and smeared like a sandwich with brown sauce. We were allowed to take a Camp coffee bottle, washed out and containing cold water. This was because the camp coffee bottle, in those days, was small and made of thick glass, which did not easily break. This proved to be effective because loads of kids I knew used them over quite a few years. I don't remember a single breakage.

We would spend hours and hours catching sticklebacks, minnows, water boatmen, water beetles, worms, butterflies, damselflies, and dragonflies. It was all fair game to us. It wasn't our intention to be cruel, but in our infantile ignorance, cruel we certainly were. The insects died fairly quickly, but we would take our jam jars, cram bang full of sticklebacks and minnows back home and put them outside on our kitchen window sill where we could admire them from within the house. We could not understand why they were all dead the next morning through lack of oxygen or, on one early spring occasion, through being frozen in ice. We persevered with this pastime for a while because the day at the pond was so enjoyable. However, the results the next day and burying dead fish eventually deterred us, and we stopped our activities.

Sticklebacks

The Farmer's Ditches

Soon after our pond expeditions, our attention turned to the Farmer's ditches. Every field was edged with a hedge and a wooden fence, next to which a drainage ditch was dug about a foot wide and a foot deep. The farmer kept these ditches nicely cleared so that they continued to provide adequate drainage for the fields. In early spring, male frogs could be heard in and around the ditches, croaking loudly to attract females for mating and warning off other male frogs from their territory. When we heard the croaking, we knew it wouldn't be long before the "spawn" came. Soon the ditches were full of frogspawn. Great gelatinous masses made up of clear tapioca-like bubbles with black dots in each one which, of course, eventually turned into tadpoles before the small proportion of them which survived became tiny frogs. The mortality rate was naturally high, and I'm afraid we kids made it even worse. Each of us would lie on our bellies above a ditch and scoop a bucketful of frogspawn and heave it up to carry home and empty into an old zinc bath or enamel bowl of water. Our desire to be surrounded by frogs blinded us to the fact that we were actually killing them.

As with the sticklebacks and minnows, after a couple of seasons, we came to the conclusion that this was not a good thing to do. In the meantime, our country-boyish curiosity led us on to Great Crested Newts, which we tickled like trout before flipping them out of the water. We did, however, very gently put these back. We were learning.

For a while, I kept a grass snake in a tank in the hedge at the bottom of our garden, but one of the older, wiser boys educated me with a simple message which I have never forgotten. "You know nowt, you bloody idiot. If you don't let it go, the poor bugger will starve to death." I'm a bit thick at times, but it dawned on me then that as I had no idea what to feed my snake, my older, wiser friend was right, and so I let it go. I have a soft side to my nature, and I felt quite sad as I watched it slither through the grass toward the cornfield. “Goodbye, Sid. I’ll miss you.”

Birds

I also became fascinated by birds at an early age. It all started when my parents bought me a beautiful blue budgerigar. We named him Billy, and I loved him. I was always an outdoors child, and when I was allowed out, I was out of that door as fast as I could. On the other hand, if the weather was really bad and I was kept in, I could always be found talking to Billy. Sometimes I even sang to him. His favourite was “Around the world. I’ve searched for you.”

We had loads of wild birds visiting our garden. Mum was quite knowledgeable and would patiently repeat the names of the birds. We had a tame Mistle Thrush (almost). It would perch upon the handlebars of an old bike that leaned on the wall in our yard. It would tilt its head sideways just like Billy the Budgie and blink its eyes if I talked to it softly. I dearly wanted it to feed from my hand but never quite managed that. However, it would come quite close to me. We also had an owl in a nearby tree. I heard it regularly as I lay in bed at night, no doubt quartering the cornfield at the back of our house for its prey. I never actually saw it. Mainly because they are largely nocturnal, and as I was a young child, I was always tucked up in bed early at night. Some of the adult neighbours, along with my Dad and my Aunt, all saw it. I don’t remember anyone actually identifying the type of owl living so close to us. At such a tender age, I wasn’t even aware that there were different types. It was just “The Owl” to me. I did, however, get to know a Barn Owl (My Favourite Bird) and also a Harris Hawk later on in life.

For my next endeavour, I cleaned up a coal riddle and propped it up at an angle in our back garden with a piece of cane about a foot long to which I attached a long length of thin string. I rubbed damp soil along the string so that it would blend in with the ground. I scattered small pieces of bread underneath the propped-up coal riddle and gently laid the string in a straight line to the corner of the house around which I lay on my belly and hid. I gently took up the slack on the string. All I had to do then was peep around the corner and wait and wait and wait and wait until, at last, after about three years, a sparrow hopped under the coal riddle to peck at a piece of bread. I yanked at the string, and the cane shot towards me, allowing the coal riddle to fall flat and trap the sparrow beneath the wire grid. I was so excited. I leaped from my hiding place and approached the coal riddle. I was excited to be able to study a wild bird at close quarters. The little creature hopped up and down, fluttering in a blind panic, trying to find a way to be free. I watched it for a second and gently lifted up the coal riddle. My eyes followed it as it took off, flew over the garden hedge, and disappeared. I didn't even get a close look at it after waiting all that time. Ah well! I was learning faster these days. I had grown to love birds and never did get into raiding nests for eggs.

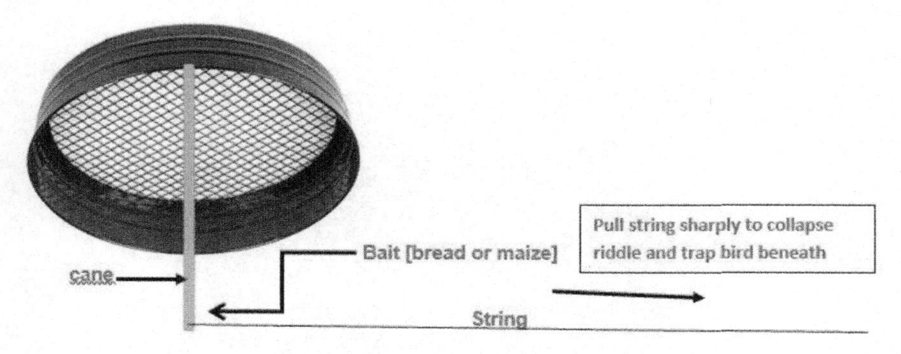

A Simple Bird Trap

(Please do not trap birds by any method. I am simply showing how, as a boy, I trapped a bird before I regretted it, learned from that and never did it again)

Dogs

I loved dogs from a very early age. There was 'Kips,' a wire-haired terrier two doors away who would bark furiously at anyone walking past his gate. Other kids gave him a wide berth, but I wasn't frit (Old Hinckley speak for frightened). I would shout "Hello, Kips" to him, and he would stop barking. Then, to my friends' horror, I would put my hand through the fence, and he would position himself for a shoulder rub. He was just a loud old softie. Then there was Judy. She was a Golden Spaniel owned by a lovely lady who went by the name of Nan Woolley. She minded me, for Mum, from time to time when I was a nipper. I would sit for ages in the side entry to her house. I would have my arm around Judy, who would happily sit with me. In those days, Mum, Dad, and I would regularly visit my Aunt Nell and Uncle Shef. Their dog, Bruce, would spend a lot of time in the backyard of their miner's cottage in Bermuda Village near Nuneaton. He wasn't chained up or anything, but he never went far. He was a big dog, and I loved him.

Landlady's Labrador

My Aunt's dog, Bruce

Biters and Stingers

I've always hated midges or gnats, as we used to call them. They always seemed to bite me more than other people. Sometimes they have bitten me extensively and not bitten people who were standing next to me. I seem to attract them. I don't know why. I shower every day. Why pick on me? Ants, on the other hand, only bite you if you bother them. A nest of ants is something to behold and very interesting to observe as long as you make sure you are not accessible to them. I could watch them for ages. Also, I have always loved bees. They will not sting you if you just keep calm and ignore them. If a bee is agitated enough by you, it will sink its sting into your flesh. However, a bee's sting is jagged, and it cannot pull it cleanly back out of you. It pulls and pulls to gain release and eventually rips the sting off, which is like ripping off a limb. It dies soon after. A bee stings once and then dies, leaving its sting in your flesh which needs to be removed with tweezers. Long before I learned how important bees are to our ecosystem, I found it such a joy to watch bees collecting pollen from flowers. People who would kill bees should remember that if it wasn't for our bees, very little would grow, including fruit and vegetables. Leave them alone, and they will rarely sting.

Wasps, on the other hand, have smooth stings and can repeatedly sting again and again. In the early 1950s, when I was a small boy, we were greatly troubled by the sheer number of wasps around our countryside home. The windows would be opened, particularly on a warm summer day and into our house, they would fly, one or two at a time, regularly all day long. If Dad got fed up with killing them by swatting them with a rolled-up newspaper, the windows would have to be closed, and we would have to suffer the stifling heat and stuffy air inside our house. It was my Dad who came up with a solution. He would leave a little jam in the bottom of a jar of jam. Put about half an inch of water in it. Then he would fix the lid back on and punch a few holes in it with a small chisel, just big enough to let in a wasp. A few of these would be strategically placed around the house, outside on the window sills near the open windows. The odd wasp still came in to do battle with Dad, but the vast majority could not resist the smell of the fruity jam and would squeeze through a hole into the jar hoping for a feast. The problem for these wasps was that they could not get back out again and would furiously buzz and hover around inside the jam jar until, eventually, their fate was sealed as their strength was depleted, and they fell and drowned in the jammy water at the bottom.

Having been stung a few times by them while playing, I hated them. More often than not, the sting would be sudden, unexpected, unprovoked and quite painful. My hatred for them was so intense that one day I very misguidedly went into battle with them. I had noticed wasps, lots of them, going in and out of a grassy clump halfway down a steep grassy bank on some nearby waste ground. I watched them from a distance to see exactly where the nest was. I had a penny banger (firework) hidden from my parents. I went home and secretly stole three matches from a box next to the gas stove. I retrieved my penny banger from its hiding place and went back to the grassy bank, picking up a stone on the way. I carefully climbed up the bank from the rear and crawled toward the edge of my belly.

Hanging over the edge and close to the bank, I struck a match on the stone and lit the penny banger. Once it was fizzing strongly, I poked it into the hole in the grey nest and quickly began to clamber back up the grassy bank. I was nowhere near back at the top of the grassy bank when it went off. **BANG**! Fragments of a wasp's nest, clumps of earth and dead wasps rained down on me, but I had not (as I expected) killed them all. There were a lot of them left, probably dazed, and they were buzzing angrily around me. I was soon down the other side of that grassy bank. I ran across the wasteland like a greyhound on roller skates but not before one of them stung me on the eyelid. Before I even went to bed that night, it swelled up as big as gooseberry, and I could see nothing at all out of that eye. Luckily it soon went down, and I fully recovered in no time. Please note that this is not a recommended pest control method. Always seek professional help. I did learn my lesson. Next time, instead of a penny banger, I used a tuppenny cannon.

Wasps Nest

Working Horses

Most of the traffic that did pass by us whilst we were playing was horse-drawn. Some books tell us that the demise of draught horses in England was in the 1930s. I beg to differ. It may have begun in the 1930s, but in the mid-to-late 1950s, our bread, milk and coal were all still delivered by horse-drawn vehicles. The field behind our home was also still ploughed by a horse-drawn ploughshare. If I close my eyes, I can still see and hear the green and yellow flatbed milk cart and the navy-blue box cart used to deliver bread. These carts were both operated from the co-op in Burbage. I can still see, in my mind's eye, the two grey horses pulling the plough for Farmer Bailey, the birds following on to see what juicy grubs, insects and worms they could grab and eat from the newly turned fold of earth and hear the calls to them as well as the rattle of chains. Eventually, at various times, these horses were all replaced by motorized trucks and tractors.

My First Fish on Rod and Line

I can recall my first time out with rod and line. My Mum was going shopping in Leicester for the day with her sister, Mavis. My Dad decided that at six years, I had reached a suitable age to be introduced to the fine malarky of fishing with rod and line. There were many skills that needed mastering, practicing and honing to perfection and much knowledge to be learned. One had to start somewhere. So it was that I found myself sitting on a towpath next to the old Coventry Road bridge close to where the Marina and Premier Inn are now. I was sitting next to Dad.

Before setting up his own tackle, he had set up a rod for me. He had threaded up the line and tied it to the bottom ring so that, for the time being, I did not even have to worry about a reel. If my float went under to indicate that a fish had made off with the maggot on the small hook attached to my line, all I had to do was give it a short, sharp tug [known as a strike], I was assured, to catch a fish. Dad tried to enthuse me, and I tried to take it all in as he waffled on and on. There were so many other things going on all around to catch my attention. Those swans, that lorry moving slowly over the bridge. A narrowboat chugging gently by on the canal. That bird sitting in the tree. I hadn't seen one like that before and look at that cow scratching its rump on the fencepost. The distractions also caused me to keep jumping up and shouting questions to Dad and running here and there to investigate this and that. In my defence, that is how my life had been lived at that time. There are many wonders to behold for a child growing up in the countryside and few restrictions of the free movement necessary for a child to explore all that caught his eye. I just was not used to sitting still and being quiet.

Dad kept telling me to sit down and be quiet, but the more he told me, the more fed up and bored I was. Then Dad got annoyed and fed up with my un-fisherman-like behaviour. He began to pack up the tackle. He was so frustrated that he left his landing net on the bank when we left to walk back to where the car was parked. Halfway back home, he realized what he had done and returned to the canal, but it was gone. Somebody had a lucky find. A brand-new net. A recent birthday present from Mum. The journey home was very quiet. My Dad was not a happy chappie.

A few weeks later, Dad went fishing without me. I can't say that I was really bothered. My first fishing trip had not inspired me or fired my enthusiasm. I spent the day in the recreation ground playing football with my mates. When I went home for my tea, my Dad had also returned. He informed me that he had 'summat to show me. He led the way to the bathroom, and there, in about ten inches of water in our bath, was a small Tench about three-quarters of a pound. It was swimming up and down the length of the bath. I watched it with interest. "Dad," I whispered, "That is beautiful," and I meant it. I thought it was, and I still do.

As was Dad's usual practice, he returned that small Tench to the canal unharmed, but not before I had watched it for quite some time and questioned my Dad about it. Dad knew what he was doing. He did not drone on about it in great detail. Instead, he drew me in by drip-feeding me with information, giving me time to digest each one, dropping out occasional little gems about Tench, their feeding habits, how big they grew to be, their fins, how he caught Tench, the line used, hook size, bait, etc. I remembered everything he said, and then I thought myself to be quite knowledgeable.

A few weeks later, he casually informed me that he was going fishing for Tench on Saturday. "Can I come, Dad? Can I come, Dad?" I chanted excitedly. "I don't know, son. You weren't very well behaved last time I took you fishing. Were you?" "Ah, but Dad, I will be now Dad cos I've got the enthoo, enthusy, en……knowledge, Dad."
"Okay," he laughed. "Just make sure you sit still and quiet, and we'll see if we can catch some Tench."

Saturday could not come soon enough for me. Dad took me to another canal. This time in Blaby. He set me up, and I caught a Tench even though it was only slightly larger than the one Dad had in the bath, they fight well, and I enjoyed the excitement of landing that beautiful fish and the feel of it struggling against my line, under Dad's guidance of course. I had foul-hooked it. Attracted to my loose feed, it had accidentally become hooked in its dorsal fin rather than its lip. Dad told me that it doesn't matter that it was foul hooked, you attracted it to your bait and loose feed and struck when your float slid away and under (a typical Tench bite), and you played it into your landing net and returned it to the water unharmed. My first fish caught on rod and line. A one-pound Tench. I was over the moon.

Tench

Early Morning Antics

Dad often went fishing with his mate from next door. I called him Uncle Jim, although he wasn't really an uncle. I called his wife, Auntie Jean. As I got a little older, I used to go fishing with Dad and Uncle Jim. They both had old cars and would take turns providing the transport. Neither car was very big. Dad's car only had a very small, one-suitcase boot. Rods were placed inside the car between the two front seats. As look would have it, they just fitted in, resting on the dashboard and touching the front screen, which Dad was able to open a little from the bottom. The other end of the fishing rods rested on a small parcel shelf and touched the rear screen. The boot dropped down, and Dad would use it as a rack by resting skips and boxes on it and making them secure with straps and string. Everything else, including thermos flasks, packed lunches, wellingtons and coats, had to be packed inside. There was only just room for me at the back. It was very tight.

As I look back, I have no idea how we got everything aboard Uncle Jim's car. It had no boot at all, but it did have a parcel rack bolted to the back end and a small roof rack. Everyone's rods were securely tied and strapped to the roof rack, and skips and boxes were likewise secured to the little parcel rack at the rear. Yes, you have guessed it, everything else went inside. I was packed in so tightly with all the kit that I could hardly breathe.

We would be up very early in the morning, often by 3.30 am. We had to be quiet so as not to wake Mum, and we knew that Uncle Jim was doing the same next door. We would have a bowl of cereal and a small cup of tea. Dad would make drinks to take with us in the thermos flasks. Now here is the thing. All that car packing described above had to be done next. There was a lot to pack and secure, and we had to be quiet. The reason that we had to do it early morning was that neither Dad nor Uncle Jim had a garage at the time, so we could not do it the night before and leave all that expensive fishing kit outside all night. It would have got nicked. Lastly, we would all go for a wee before setting off. House doors were locked and keys were pushed through the letter box for the women-folk to pick up. The car would be started, and each of the occupants would hold a door open until we were well up the road. We would all then slam the doors shut, thereby running the risk of waking local people up but not our own folk and near neighbors.

This rigmarole, as you may imagine, caused a problem or two. I remember Uncle Jim locking his house door and pushing the house key through the letterbox. We were going in his car that day, and as he returned to us sitting in his car, he began to pat his pockets. He could not find his car keys. Then he remembered that he had left them on the kitchen table. He had to go back and wake Auntie Jean up. Dad and I stayed where we were. We knew Auntie Jean would be livid. Boy, was Uncle Jim in trouble. I don't remember anyone having spare keys in those days. I don't know why.

Another early morning saw us loaded up to the gunwales (as my Dad used to say). Again, we were going in Uncle Jim's car, but my Dad was driving it this day, partly because he was an experienced driver and Uncle Jim had only recently passed his test and partly because Dad knew the way better than Uncle Jim. (I cannot remember specifically where we were going) Anyway, Dad settled himself behind the wheel and decided to softy shut his door onto the first latch (to be slammed shut up the road). The trouble was that he had forgotten that the horn button on Uncle Jim's car was not in the center of the steering wheel but stuck out sideways to the right of the steering column. As Dad shut the door, it trapped his knee between the door and the horn button.

BEEEEEEEEEEEEEEEEEEEEEEEEEEEEEEEEEEEEEEEP!

All our efforts not to wake people up had been wasted. Dad and Jim looked at each other in horror as Dad struggled to open the door in order to release the horn button and stop that awful noise. After about six months, he managed it but rapidly started the car, and we shot up the road as fast as that little car would go. Then we all slammed our doors shut. Dad explained the reason for our sharp take-off was that if the horn woke up the womenfolk, they would look out of the window. If they didn't actually see us, we could deny responsibility and swear that we had left ages before that. It worked. We got away with it for once.

One winter morning saw us in Jim's car again, on our way to Northamptonshire to do a spot of fishing. It was very early and pitch dark. The old Morris 8 was popping along about 45 mph when from normal, the beam from the headlights got brighter and brighter like searchlights and lit up the whole area like daylight, and then just as suddenly, **PHUT**! Went out altogether. It was most disconcerting as we were still speeding along but couldn't even see the end of the bonnet. Uncle Jim bought the car screeching to a halt as far to the left as he dared. Whatever caused it could not be fixed, so we had to wait there until it was light enough to carry on without lights. We had to make sure we left the fishing venue in time to get home before darkness fell, and Uncle Jim got it mended the next day.

Fishing with my Mate Bill

I think I was about twelve or thirteen years old when I met a lad at 1st Burbage Scouts by the name of Alan Smith, who was about a year older than me. His nickname was Bill. Nobody but his parents called him Alan. He lived in Sketchley Road Burbage. After "Scouts" on a Friday evening, a lot of the lads would pile around to the chip shop on Windsor Street. One night, while we were waiting to get served, Bill was next to me in the queue, and we got talking about fishing. It turned out he was an enthusiastic angler, and we made arrangements for Bill to come to our house down Banky Meadow on the following day. We grew to be really good mates, and over the next few years, we enjoyed fishing together as well as all sorts of other activities. We went swimming once a week and quite often to the cinema. We attended guitar lessons together. Occasionally, we would watch a local football team. We went hiking, camping, and bird watching together as well as occasional outings such as Scout events, funfairs, etc. I got on well with his parents. His Mother, in particular, was a lovely lady. My parents liked him too, so we were around each other's houses quite often. Bill would sometimes come on family outings and family holidays with me. We shared the same kind of humour and had many good laughs as we grew up.

Sadly, Bill moved out of the area with his job, and we lost touch. I don't even know, as I write this, whether he is still alive or not. I look back at the times we had together with great fondness. He was the best mate I ever had.

Me (left) and my mate Bill Smith on holiday in Norfolk in the mid - 1960s.

Anyway, back to the fishing. Bill and I must have fished every stretch of Canal within a fifteen-mile radius of Hinckley. We would strap our rods to our bicycle cross bars. I had a parcel rack over my rear wheel, to which I secured my tackle box. Bill preferred to carry his tackle in a rucksack on his back. We both had yellow oilskin cycle capes, which incorporated head covers, so even if it rained, we would still go fishing. We would regularly rise early and cycle miles to fish canals.

Burton Hastings Canal

The Ashby Canal runs through Hinckley, so Bill and I fished it quite often, particularly if we only had a few hours to fish. I clearly remember at one point in time. We used to go down to the canal near the Lime Kilns on the A5 and sell maggots to anglers who had rushed from work for a couple of hours fishing and hadn't had time to go into the town to buy maggots. We didn't sell them for cash, though. One good handful cost the lucky fishermen one cigarette. "Thanks, Lads, but don't tell your Dads I gave you that fag" was a line we heard quite often. We were seasoned smokers by the time we were fourteen.

We fished the canal near Burton Hastings Village more often than anywhere because it was a lovely place out in the countryside, which we preferred to the Town. We spent hours on many a day, all year round, sitting there pitting our wits against the fish. Drinking coffee from our flasks, eating our sandwiches and having a puff of a cigarette from time to time. In the winter, we would go fishing for pike. Three and a half pounds was my biggest, but I caught quite a lot that weighed in at around the two pounds to two and a half pounds mark. Sometimes we used to spin for pike and perch. Other times we would use the live bait and dead bait methods.

Early one morning, we arrived at Burton Hastings Canal on our bikes. As usual, we were loaded up with tackle and provisions. As I rode behind Bill, he must have hit a pothole in the towpath, but from my point of view, it looked as if he had made a decision to suddenly turn sharp left and cycle directly into the canal. I was shocked. I braked, jumped off my bike and immediately began taking off all the layers of coats and jumpers I had put on to keep warm. I was ready to jump in to help if Bill was in difficulties. [I was a recently certificated grade three lifesaver and a very strong swimmer] I could see Bill's bike. It was about a foot underwater but lying flat and horizontal. What scared me was that I couldn't see Bill. I knew that the water was only about three feet deep at that point, but I also knew that there was up to a foot of soft mud at the bottom, which could literally bog you down. I also know that Bill had his rucksack on his back to weigh him down. I was still taking off layers when I saw his rucksack appear, obviously being pushed up and sideways out of the way by Bill. Then Bill's head popped up, and he gasped and drew a deep breath. One wheel of his bike was near to me, so I pulled it towards me, and Bill grabbed the frame, and I helped to pull him in. His rucksack came close to me, and I grabbed that, hauled it up and dropped it onto the towpath. As the bike grounded itself, I let go and grabbed Bill's outstretched hand.

I fell backward onto my bottom as he emerged, dripping from the canal. He was covered in brown mud and green slime and smelled pretty bad. It was a cold, wet ride back to Burbage for Bill. His Mother took his dirty clothes for washing, and he disappeared upstairs to have a hot bath. I went out into the yard and gave his bike a hose down with his Dad's garden hose. I opened up his rucksack and, item by item, dried and cleaned up his fishing tackle the best I could using old towels. After a while, he came downstairs in clean clothes, and his Mum gave us both a steaming mug of hot tea and a few ginger biscuits each. We began to talk about the incident and, being young lads, soon ended up roaring with laughter about it. When I told him that I wondered why he decided to turn left into the canal without signalling, Bill laughed hysterically. The main thing is that Bill was alright after his ordeal.

Blaby Canal

We often used to cycle to our favourite spot, on Blaby Canal, with our fishing tackle. It was a twenty-five-mile round trip, but we were both sturdy young chaps and pretty fit back then. There are two incidents from our trips to Blaby that I particularly remember. We had been fishing there for a long time one day and hadn't caught much. Just a couple of very small perch each. This was unusual. Bill's float began to bob about in the water. Bill picked up his rod. He wasn't "striking" to drive the hook home because he knew it was a tiddler. He hooked it anyway and was reeling it in when a small jack pike with wide open jaws suddenly made a grab for the tidder and somehow managed to get itself hooked. It must be appreciated that we used a very light line and tackle when we fished the canal, so when the jack pike took off, Bill had to be careful that the force did not break the line, or the fish would be lost. There was also the danger that the jack pike would bite through the line and escape. Bill played the fish in just right and was really rather pleased with his jack pike.

Another time we set out to cycle to Blaby in the early morning sunshine. We arrived and set up and had a pretty good morning's sport. Both of us caught quite a few Roach and Perch. We ate our packed lunch and noticed that the morning sun had disappeared. The sky had become quite black, and a fairly strong wind had got up. Our light canal tackle had become difficult to handle in the wind, which was getting stronger. We decided to pack up. We secured our tackle to our bikes and set off for home. Suddenly, the rain came. It hammered down. We had our oilskin capes on, but our legs were getting soaked and cold, and the wind had become so strong that we were concerned we could be blown off our bikes. It was definitely dodgy.

We sheltered in a bus shelter for a while, but it didn't look like abating. We rummaged through our pockets to see what money we had. The canal bailiff had not ventured out to collect our day-ticket money, so we had a little cash between us for once. We headed for the Railway Station. Spoke to the Station Master there and explained what had happened. We told him how much cash we had and asked him if it was enough to get back to Hinckley. "I'm afraid you don't have enough lads."

By now, it was a proper rainstorm and almost blowing a gale. He looked at us thoughtfully. "Follow me" he yelled to us and led us onto the platform, and pointed to the guard's van. It was about half full of boxes.

"Put your bikes in there," he said, "and if you travel with them, I'll just charge you for a ticket each for yourselves and not the bikes. Then you have enough, see?"

We thanked him profusely and did as he suggested. The storm had calmed down by the time we got to Hinckley, so our legs were damp, but we had arrived home safe and sound.

A jack pike (Young Pike) like the one Bill caught

Shenton Canal Bend

Bill and I fished Shenton Canal a lot. At one point, it goes over an aqueduct with the road underneath. Here we sometimes caught crayfish. It wasn't really intentional. We would be fishing for Roach and Perch or perhaps hoping to catch a Tench. Of course, back then, we encountered NATIVE crayfish. Sadly, some idiot introduced the American Signal Crayfish to UK waters. These are bigger and much more aggressive than our native species. The same thing happened when another idiot introduced American Grey Squirrels to the UK. Our beautiful native Red Squirrel almost became extinct. Our native Crayfish is going the same way, and don't even mention to me the know-nothing, interfering, gormless imbeciles who released hundreds of attractive but vicious American Mink from captivity in the name of animal rights. Years later, these savage creatures still kill thousands of birds, field mice, voles and all sorts of other creatures.

I recall several times Bill and I camping overnight, on summer nights on the wide towpath on Shenton Bend. We would fish for hours on end in the warm sunshine, make tea, cook simple meals on my Dad's GAZ camp stove and sleep in Bill's old tattered Egyptian cotton tent. It was falling to bits, but it was all we had at that time. Sometimes we felt the need for some exercise and would go for a long walk or bike ride in the countryside. We didn't have much money but shared whatever we had and were having the time of our lives. One morning we were woken early by the sound of Friesian cattle paddling about in the mud and shallow water and being very vocal at a "cattle drink" on the opposite side of the canal to our tent. It was 5.30 am. We decided to get up. Bill rolled up the brailing's on our tent to let fresh air into it while I got the billy-can going to make some tea. We watched the cattle as we drank. They drank, too, from the canal. After a while, the cattle drifted away to different parts of the huge field. We decided to have a bit of exercise before we began fishing, so after our breakfast and ablutions, we went for a walk, not too far. About a mile or so around the edge of a couple of fields. When we returned to our tent, we noticed that the Friesians had disappeared, and just to the left of the cattle drink were a mother shorthorn cow and her beautiful calf. What a treat. I had my camera with me and took a photo. Fishing is not just about catching fish. It's about breathing fresh air in the countryside and observing flora and fauna and, yes what's going on at the farms too.

Mother and son. How good to see.

Cosgrove Lakes

Often we would go further afield for our sport with my Dad, Grandad and Uncle Jim. Bill and I used to fish at Cosworth Lakes in Buckinghamshire with my Dad. When we fished in the 1960s, there were lakes with a single water inlet. Today it has been extensively developed into a luxury caravan and leisure activity park. Back in the 1960s, it was hugely wooded with lots of undergrowth. We always tried to fish away from Dad's chosen spot so we could smoke the odd cigarette. We were still underage, and he would not have approved. Dad was a pipe smoker in those days, and sometimes we only located him from the odd puff of black smoke rising from the undergrowth and the pleasant aroma of St Bruno Flake tobacco.

My main memory from fishing this vast and mixed fishery was when Bill and I decided to fish the inlet, which was like a small, gently flowing river, about two feet deep by about twenty feet wide. Again, we were a good distance from where Dad was fishing, so we got set up to catch small to medium size fish. Once we were "in" we lit up a cigarette each. We were just enjoying a smoke when Bill's float shot under the water. Bill quickly stuck his fag between his lips and gently struck. He was immediately into a decent-sized roach which gradually tired, allowing Bill to wind it in towards his strategically placed landing net. Bill removed the fag from his mouth and, in doing so, accidentally burned straight through his line near the reel. Suddenly the fish darted downstream, taking three yards of Bill's line and his float with it. There was no way to retrieve the fish, or so I thought. To my amazement, Bill, determined not to lose his lovely Roach, or his float, dropped his rod and waded out into the middle of the inlet and made a grab for his float. Wrapping the line around his hand and winding up the slack, he could feel the fish fighting. I eventually closed my mouth, and Bill landed his Roach, disgorged the hook and admired it before returning it to the water. It was a lovely Roach and in really top condition. Luckily, it was a sunny day, so Bill's trousers soon dried off and spread on brambles in the sun while Bill fished for an hour or so dressed only in a shirt and his underpants. There's dedication for you.

The Grand Union Canal

One year in the mid- 1960s, instead of the usual annual camp, 1st Burbage Scouts hired two narrowboats, Crane and Warbler, in which we ate and slept as we gently chugged down the Grand Union Canal from the boatyard at Braunstone in Northamptonshire down to Leyton Buzzard in Bedfordshire. This was something new to us, and as much as we all loved camping, this was both an exciting and enjoyable change from tradition.

We had lots of fun along the way. Somewhere along this route, I cannot remember where, we were allowed a short time "ashore" in some town or other, where we came across a toyshop. Standing in a bucket outside were children's fishing nets. A small wire enclosed around a light fabric net attached to a five-foot-long cane. It was the cane that attracted the attention of my mate Bill Smith. He removed the net from one and held the cane in his hand. "You could land a one-pound (in weight) fish on this," he announced, "but will there be a tackle shop in this town to get line, shots, a quill float and some small hooks?"

There was. We even got maggots. We stowed our canes and tackle on the narrow boat. After our 'shore leave, we returned to our narrowboats, and soon we were sedately chugging along into the open countryside, and by early evening, we were moored in the quiet countryside in the middle of nowhere. We attached some lines to our canes, slid on a light quill float and tied on a small hook. We then pinched some small shots onto the line in order to make the float 'cock' (stand vertically in the water) and a small shot about six inches from the hook to sink the bait. For bait, we had maggots from the tackle shop and bread, which we scrounged from the small galley store on our narrowboat.

For the rest of the week, whenever we had the chance, Bill and I went fishing. I have wonderful memories of sitting bankside on warm summer days and evenings, catching fish, mainly Roach and Rudd but with the occasional Gudgeon and Perch. Some were quite small but catching any fish using such primitive tackle seemed somehow very satisfying and gave us a sense of achievement.

The one outstanding incident I remember to this day was when we were fishing in a place where, as we sat facing the canal, there was a very steep bank that dropped behind us almost vertically for about fifteen feet. Because we were only using a fixed and short length of line, when we struck, a small fish would occasionally leave the water and come flying towards us through the air. One evening Bill's float shot under like a rocket. Bill struck quite sharply, and as a decent-sized Roach came flying through the air towards him, he slipped and fell backward down the steep bank, still holding his cane, and disappeared from view. I ran over to the bank, and there was Bill lying full length where he had landed. He had slightly winded himself and was gasping. The funny thing was that he had somehow, amazingly, caught the Roach in his other hand as he fell, and that was also opening and closing its mouth just like Bill was. Once I realized that Bill was ok, I laughed and laughed, and after a bit of grumpy muttering and growling, Bill saw the funny side and joined in with us.

In the summer, Bill and I would often cycle home from school, pick up our fishing tackle and a pre-prepared packed tea and then cycle to various points on the Ashby Canal and go fishing for a few hours until dark or a pre-determined time. Some other kids at our school would do the same, and quite often, an unplanned fishing match would manifest itself as friends met up and threw out a challenge. Matches were sometimes individual or pairs. The competition would be taken very seriously even though the winner might only win a cigarette or a threepenny bit or occasionally a tanner (sixpence).

One day in my memory, sees Bill and I cycle down Wykin Lane to the canal. We set up in spots only about ten feet apart. We were still 'fine tuning' our tackle when two other kids turned up with fishing tackle and began to set up not far along the bank from us. They were both named Mick, but the smaller lad was nicknamed Lofty. Well, we just had to throw down a challenge to them. One fag per head, and most fish takes it all. (Sometimes, it was the weight of the fish) 'Pairs,' it was agreed (us against them). Match rules, including finish time, always had to be debated and verbally agreed upon beforehand. I whistled and bought my hand down sharply, and the match began. I think we had three hours.

After a couple of hours, we had caught a few and placed them carefully in a keepnet ready for counting at the end of the match, but we suspected that they had caught quite a few more than us. Bill told me that he would go and try to find out how many they had caught. More often than not, this information would not be revealed until the official count at the end of the match, but it's worth a try, Bill informed me as he strolled over to have a chat with the competition. (This would not be allowed in a proper official match.) Now Bill was no mug, and he knew that Mick was frightened to death of wasps. Consequently, when Mick told him to "Bugger off" and refused to give away their count of fish caught, Bill shrugged and went as if to walk back to our spot. Suddenly he yelled out, "Watch out. There's a wasp on your neck" In one movement, Mick screamed and leaped from his seat, high into the air. Interestingly, he was still in a sitting position when he hit the water. Pandemonium ensued. Mick had to be pulled out. He was still scared that a wasp was waiting to pounce. A shouting match broke out between Lofty and Bill. They were trading insults. Lofty called Bill a cheating bastard and squared up to him. As Bill was about a foot taller than Lofty, it was perhaps as well that I was there. I was shouting at both of them to give me a hand pulling Mick out of the canal. He was struggling to get a grip. When he did, he was in the right state. Covered in green slime and stinking black mud, he looked a very sorry sight indeed. Lofty packed up his own kit and then Mick's. With one withering look back at Bill and me, Lofty led his friend as he squelched up the towpath towards home.

"Shall we have a smoke now? Asked Bill. "We nearly lost our last two fags there." "Lofty was right, you know," I said as I lit a fag. "You are a cheating bastard." "Not at all," insisted Bill. "There was a wasp. I didn't dream that he would overreact, so." Bill grew up to be a very honest and honourable adult who always played fair. I guess I'll never know whether there was a wasp or whether, on that one particular occasion, Bill's schoolboy competitiveness got the better of him. As usual, we ended up laughing. This time at Mick landed in the water with a huge splash, still in the sitting position. Poor old Mick.

Camp Dadlington

This story began when I made a trailer for my bike in metalwork classes at school. It was to carry a camping and fishing kit. In order to try it out, Bill and I planned its maiden voyage. Before the trailer was even road-ready, we cycled in a north-Westerly direction, about four miles from Hinckley, to a crossroads near Dadlington. Just up the lane, from there, we approached a farm. Several farm dogs all began to bark their warning, and the Farmer appeared from nowhere. We explained that we were boy scouts (which always gives you a good start) and that we were looking for somewhere to camp and fish. We had done our homework, and we knew that the canal was only a ten-minute walk across this farmer's fields. He agreed to allow us to camp on the small field in front of the farmhouse. There was an old but polished 6-berth caravan at one side where a young blonde lady resided with her baby. In the end, near the farm entrance, there were two caravans and two lorries. These belonged to a travelling family.

The time came, and we cycled over to our farm campsite, taking turns to pull the trailer. It was loaded up with camping gear and fishing gear and food etc. We arrived without mishap and set up our tent in the exact location as instructed by the Farmer. We laid out our bedrolls in Bill's old tent. It really was showing signs of age now, partly discoloured with some of the cotton loops for guy lines, etc., worn right through. We had to do a first-aid job with string in order to make it secure. It also had several holes in the side, but it was the only tent we had. We were there for three days and two nights. We were soon at the canal side fishing and returned in the evening. As we passed by the caravan at the side of the farmhouse, we noticed the young blonde lady was outside. Well, she was very attractive. She was sitting in a chair in her small garden and enjoying the last of the dying sun's rays. She shouted a greeting, and we put down our fishing tackle to talk to her. She was really friendly, and we chatted and laughed with her for ten minutes or so before making our way back to our tent. For some silly reason which I cannot remember, Bill called her Foo-Foo. As far as we were concerned, that was her name. We camped there several times and saw quite a lot of her and, on one occasion, even babysat for her for an hour. Her real name has been swallowed up in the mists of time. She was always Foo-Foo to us. We turned up for a camp there for about the fifth time, and she had gone, and so had the caravan.

The Travellers were always nice and friendly towards us too. On our very first day, one of them came a walk over to say hello. His name was Trevor Tipper, and he explained that he was head of the family, which occupied two quality stainless steel caravans with engraved windows. He had a carrier bag and explained that some younger members of the family had been spud-picking. They were paid a small wage and allowed to keep a small number of potatoes. To our surprise, he gave us four large potatoes for our supper, and we thanked him before he also gave us two apples each. He was very friendly and jovial, gently poking fun at us but with a twinkle in his eye and without malice. Always gently joking about the proverbial fish that was 'this big' (stretching his arms wide apart) but got away. We liked him.

The next morning, I awoke early (about six 'o'clock) to feel someone waggling my feet and legs about in my sleeping bag. I must have been wriggling about whilst I was asleep, and only my head and upper body were actually in the tent. From my chest down, I was outside the tent under the tent doors, which were still tied closed. I quickly untied them and peeped out to see it was Trevor, our traveller friend. He was amused but also said it looked like rain and didn't want me or my sleeping bag to get wet. He was such a nice man. Bill woke up at the slight commotion, and we put the kettle on for tea. It wasn't a very nice day. We took our oilskin waterproofs and fishing umbrellas and did a bit of fishing. We caught a few Roach and Perch. It was quite blustery and worsened during the day to the point where it was difficult to control our lines. We stuck it until about 4.00 pm and decided to call it a day. On the way back, we had a brief chat with Foo-Foo, and she invited us to tea in her caravan.

When we got back to camp, we realized that we could be in for a right proper stormy night, so we packed everything away, secured in the trailer and checked all the guy ropes on the tent. We did our best to stop the rain from coming in through the holes in the side by plugging them up the best we could with our socks. By the time we went back to Foo Foo's caravan, the storm was raging. The wind howled, and the rain lashed down. It was very pleasant to be in a caravan with a heater on. Foo-Foo produced a tin of corned beef and asked Bill to open it for her. She then made us sandwiches and gave us a bag of crisps and a mug of tea each, and we shared a plate full of assorted biscuits for afters. Simple fare but very enjoyable. We were grateful for the hospitality. We watched TV for a while and then thanked Foo Foo for her kindness and ran as fast as we could through the heavy rain to our tent.

The water had seeped in and soaked into our bedding. Looks like we were going to have an uncomfortable night. Suddenly we heard our Romany friend shouting through the noise of the storm. He was saying that one of their lorries was a covered one. “Sleep in the back there,” he yelled, pointing to the vehicle “hard surface but nice and dry.” Bless him, we thought and thanked him, but as we made our way towards the lorry, a car made its way up the drive and swung around onto our campsite, lighting it up with the headlights. It was my Dad. He had come to fetch us home because of the bad weather. We loaded up his car but left the tent there. Trevor wheeled our bikes under a lean-to shelter he had fashioned, then pushed my trailer underneath one of their lorries, out of sight and also dry. We thanked him profusely and told him that we would return the next day. We were soaked.

The next day the storm had passed, and it was quite a nice day. My Dad gave us a lift back to the farm. The Tipper family was nowhere to be seen, and both lorries were absent. Bill's tent was ruined. A huge tear had appeared. We rolled it up and placed it in my trailer, which I had retrieved from beneath the lean-to. After we had returned and Bill had gone home, I had a nice surprise. My Dad told me that he thought it was good that Bill and I followed our outdoor pursuits like camping and fishing. For that reason, I am going to buy you a decent tent that will stand up to bad weather, he informed me. He was true to his word. I became the proud owner of a really good tent complete with flysheet. We never had to come home again, and as I grew up, that tent went with various mates all over the UK and me. I think I was about twenty years old when I eventually threw it out. It was worn out by then. I certainly had Dad's money's worth out of it.

Sunday Morning Dip

A few weeks later, we had a Sunday morning fishing trip. This time we went mob-handed. We rose very early, and I and Dad went over to fetch my Grandad from Earl Shilton and returned to meet my mate Ian and his Dad, Jim) at the canal at Dadlington. We all sat on the towpath in a line. In those days, the canals contained plenty of small species such as roach, perch, gudgeon and bullhead (millers thumb), and these were pretty easy to catch. Also, there was always the chance of a larger roach or perch or, best of all, Tench. There were also pike lurking in the reeds, but different fishing methods were used to catch these. Dad set me up, and I sat watching my float, waiting for it to bob or disappear into the water to indicate that a fish had taken my bait.

After an hour or so, I noticed that nobody had caught anything, and I began to get a little restless. I had already wolfed down a cold bacon sandwich for breakfast, washed down with a lovely hot cup of coffee out of my Dad's thermos flask. I had looked around a bit

for birds, but there was not much nature to witness on that particular morning.
“Come on, fish,” I shouted in my head. “Bloody BITE” Another half-hour dragged slowly by. I was sitting on a wooden fishing box my Dad had made for me, and as I fidgeted, I kept tilting it forward, stretching my legs out in front of me. Suddenly, as I tilted it forward for the umpteenth time, my feet slipped over the edge of the canal towpath, and I slid off my box like a plank, feet first into the cold water up to my waist. It took my breath away, I can tell you. I turned and tried to pull myself back up the bank. My Dad was there in a flash and, grabbing my outstretched hand, pulled me out of the canal. I won’t repeat what he called me. He was really annoyed. He, indeed all of us, had only a few hours to enjoy a bit of sport and fresh air, and now he had to waste the best part of an hour taking me back home to dry and change my clothes. I cannot say that Mum was impressed either. Looking back, though, I do remember that everyone else had a chuckle about my “dip,” especially Jim and my Grandad.

We returned to find that the sun had strengthened and warmed the water a little with the result that fish had begun to feed, and the rest of the party had all caught at least a couple of fish. Encouraged by this, I got down to it and was rewarded with several roach and a perch all around the half-pound mark. All too soon, we had to pack up and take Grandad back and return to our Burbage home for Sunday Lunch. Quite a successful morning, I thought.

The Ashby Canal

The River Soar at Leicester

I used to fish the River Soar at Leicester quite a lot in the mid - the 1960s. A section of the river flowing through the city is canalized. We approached it from Western Boulevard. The buildings on the East and West bank were totally different then. On the West bank, there was a huge yard belonging to a plant hire company. I think it was called Berry's. On the East bank, there was some sort of factory that regularly discharged warm water into the river, downstream of which was good fishing. I first started to fish there with my Dad. Sometimes my Grandad Perkins came along. When I was about fourteen, I used to cycle there with my mate Bill Smith. Despite being in the city, it was quite a pleasant place to fish, the only trouble being that the concrete bank meant that you could not get a rod rest or a bank stick into the ground.

There are two memories that stand out to me. The first one was Dad, Bill, and I decided to fish there on the opening day of the fishing season (16th June). We arrived at about 10:30 pm on the 15th of June in plenty of time to get three pegs together and set up our kit ready for midnight. There was a long line of anglers stretched along the bank for quite a long way. Midnight came, and as the local church began to chime twelve times, they all picked up their rods and cast in at the same time. I glanced lengthways down the West bank, and the rods were almost synchronized. It reminded me of the Tiller Girls. Just after that, the street lights went out.

Most of us wanted to cast our bait over near the opposite bank. It wasn't easy as it was very dark and shadowy over there. We developed a system whereby you would cast and try and judge where the opposite bank was. If you heard a splash, you knew your bait was in the water, but if you heard a thud, you had hit the bank, and so you would reel in and try again. One year we fished in a spot opposite the old-fashioned blue police box. At about 2:00 am, we saw a policeman cycling along on the opposite bank. He stopped and unlocked the police box, probably to make a phone call. Bill had re-baited his hook and cast out towards the bank and listened for a splash or a thud. He must have been a bit heavy-handed because what we all heard was a BANG as Bill's leger weight hit the blue police box. The policeman appeared from the box and looked around. We couldn't see his face, but I bet he wore a puzzled look as Bill gently wound the leger back in again.

Another memory is of a lovely sunny morning. I was fishing at our favourite spot with my Dad and my Grandad. Suddenly the end of my rod whipped right around. I struck, and immediately, I could tell I had hooked into a decent carp. They are really strong fighters. While I was playing it in, I became aware that my Grandad, to my right, was also playing a fish. After playing with the fish for a few minutes, we all realized that my line and Grandad's line formed a vee shape as they appeared to join up in the middle of the river. We knew straightaway that only one of us had caught the carp, and the other had foul-hooked the other person's line. My Grandad shouted that he thought the fish was his, but as the words left his lips, his line went slack. The fish was mine. Soon I had a beautiful three-and-a-half-pound common carp on the bank. I was so chuffed. Grandad was disappointed that it wasn't him who had caught the fish, but he was always a sportsman. He and my Dad both came and admired it. Patted me on the back and told me, "Well done." I was grinning like a Cheshire cat.

The canalized River Soar in Leicester

Knossington Lake

There was a period when I was around seven years old when my Grandad, Dad and I would drive over to Knossington Lake. It was at the back of a farm just outside the village. The lake itself was beautiful and long-established. There were Lilly-pads along one side, and the lake was surrounded by trees in a beautiful woodland setting. As we carried our kit from the car park and followed the path down to the lake, we passed a brick-built pigsty. Expecting it to be empty, I peered over the wall into the pigsty, and there was this enormous pig. We would all spend a few minutes saying "hello" to her, and she would softly grunt as if returning our meeting. She would respond when we said "Tara" on our way back to the car. It became part of our day out, which we all enjoyed.

My Grandad loved it there. Sometimes he would come with us, arriving at the lake at about 5:30 am. Other times, his brother, my Great Uncle Les, would bring him and arrive about 7:00 am I don't remember Uncle Les actually fishing himself. He just enjoyed a ride out into the country and sitting with Grandad in the fresh air. It was Grandad's sort of venue. An old-fashioned Lilly-pond type of place, and he was in his element. He knew how to fish it, and although we considered his fishing tackle to be outdated, he usually caught more fish than anyone else at this particular venue despite giving us the hour-and-a-half start when he came with brother Les.

I loved it there too. I would throw a handful of maggots to the side of the Lilly pads every now and then and load a size ten hook with a big bunch of maggots. My Mum had thoughtfully packed me plenty of sandwiches with crisps and a couple of wafers, along with a Beano comic in case I got bored. No chance. By the time Grandad and Great Uncle Les arrived, I had seven Tench in my keepnet from one to two pounds in weight. I had also been smashed. That is to say, a huge fish, probably a carp or a huge Tench, broke my line. The fish would feed for a while, then either go off the feed or perhaps were patrolling around the lake in shoals as fish tend to do and would return in due course to the area I was fishing, and I would start to catch again. I couldn't believe it at the end of the day when Grandad had caught me up with the quantity of fish, but since, on average, mine were a bit bigger than his, Great Uncle Les declared it a draw. What a lovely day out. We did it again and again.

On one occasion, Dad and I travelled over there, and about a mile away from our destination, the bracket at the back end of the exhaust pipe failed and dragged along the lane, sounding like a car crash. Dad lay on his back and looked under the car. The exhaust pipe itself was in quite a good condition. It was just the bracket holding it up that had broken. Dad retrieved his pliers from the car, and we headed towards the farm fencing. We only wanted a couple of strips about four inches long. It wasn't as if the fence would fall down or allow animals to escape. We had obtained our wire and were returning to the car when we were suddenly surprised by the Farmer who came hurtling around the corner in his Land Rover.

When he saw us, he stopped and got out. By now, Dad had pushed the wire and the pliers into the huge poacher's pocket in his Barbour coat. The Farmer asked if everything was OK? Luckily he didn't notice the exhaust pipe on the ground. Dad assured him that we were just answering the call of nature. The two adults exchanged pleasantries for a minute or so, mainly about the weather and the Farmer got back into his vehicle and, with a wave, drove off. Dad soon carried out a first aid job, fastening the exhaust to its anchor with the wire and off we went to catch more Tench. We often had a laugh about the time we could easily have been in trouble with the Farmer who nearly caught us out at five ' o'clock one morning.

Somewhere in Buckinghamshire

Early in 1963, Mum told me that my Dad had booked a fishing holiday for the three of us in Buckinghamshire. I cannot for the life of me remember exactly where it was. (I was only 12 years old) Somewhere South of Leighton Buzzard is all I remember Dad saying. Anyway, we stayed in a railway carriage, which had been beautifully converted to living quarters. It even had a bath. The toilet, however, was at the rear of a huge house just a short walk from the railway carriage. The big house had a big garden which ran down to the water's edge where we were allowed to fish. I seem to remember it was an arm of a tributary to the River Ouse. Across the river were a shallow valley and a huge grass bank leading upwards to a busy railway line. Trains passed up and down all day long. They were close enough to see but not close enough for the noise to get on our nerves.

I set up with fairly light tackle, and every day of the holiday, I would catch plenty of small fish ranging from small Bleak and Dace to larger Skimmer Bream, Roach, and Rudd up to about three-quarters of a pound. Good sport for a young lad. Dad geared up to catch bigger fish which is generally more of a waiting game. Dad caught fewer fish but bigger ones. He netted several Bream to four and a half pounds and a three-pound Perch.

Apart from enjoying the fishing, my main memory of the holiday was my sense of absolute shock and awe when I switched on the small black and white television set in our 'living quarters' to learn that a daring and audacious but well-planned train robbery had taken place not far from where we were staying. The robbers got away with £2.6 Million pounds in used notes after stopping the Glasgow to London Royal Mail train at Bridego Railway Bridge (since renamed Mentmore Bridge) near Ledburn in Buckinghamshire. At today's value, as I write, in 2022, the haul was worth over £56 Million. I was shocked again and even more in awe when Dad told me that we probably saw the train go by whilst we were fishing. At twelve years old, that was a big WOW!

Our carriage awaited

I've caught another one, Dad

Me and my Dad enjoying ourselves

Barwell Lane Pit

For years this pit, known locally as the Little Pit (to distinguish it from a bigger pit nearby, funnily enough, known locally as the Big Pit), has belonged to Hinckley Angling Club for many years. Near the edge of the town (Hinckley), it is bordered by trees and undergrowth. There are about twenty pegs. It runs to about twenty feet deep. When I was about twelve or thirteen, Dad made us both members of the club. It was handy, particularly in the summer. When Dad was on the morning shift, he finished at 2:00 pm and would prepare everything and load the fishing kit into the car along with a bag containing a packed tea and a flask of coffee. He would pick me up from school at home time, and off we would go to the Little Pit and fish until late evening.

My best memory of these times concerns a tree. One summer evening, we were fishing in the Little Pit. I had just changed my bait and was about to cast it back in. However, on the backswing, I got snagged quite high up in a tree. I tried to gently free my tackle from the tree with no success. I called my Dad, who was fishing quite close by. He couldn't reach the hook, which was stuck fast.

"Pull the branch down, Den, so I can reach the hook." I did a little jump up and grabbed the offending branch, then hung on it to pull it down with my weight to Dad's eye level. He got hold of the hook and was trying to pull it free when I slipped and let go of the branch, which shot back up, driving the hook deep into Dad's thumb. "Ooyah bugger," shouted Dad, who was now dancing about on tip-toe with his arm stretched upwards and his hooked thumb in the air. "Get it back down, you silly sod."

Unfortunately, by now, I couldn't move for laughing and was unable to immediately come to his aid. He continued shouting, cursing and dancing, and jumping up and down on tip-toe as he made wild sideway swipes with his free hand, no doubt in the hope that one of them would connect with my earhole. Seeing as I was causing him so much pain, he naturally felt the need to cause me some back. Having hooked a digit or two myself, I knew how painful it was, but to have the upward pressure of the branch driving it into his flesh must have been agony.

I recovered from my hysterics enough to jump up again and pull the branch down while Dad freed himself. Luckily for me, in doing so, the hook had fallen free. Dad kept sucking his thumb and was grumpy for the rest of the evening. I'm afraid to report that the whole episode cheered me up no end, and I kept having to turn away from him as I tried not to let him see me laughing every few minutes for the rest of the evening, including when I went to bed. I just couldn't drop off to sleep because I couldn't stop laughing. Aren't kids cruel? Even now, sixty years later, I often recall the image of Dad dancing on tip-toe and chuckle to myself.

Norfolk Broads

During the mid – the 1960s, we spent a lot of holiday time and weekends on the Norfolk coast. Especially after my Dad bought a caravan and stationed it at the Wild Duck Caravan Park at Belton. We used to get up early and fish the nearby broads and return for lunch and then take the womenfolk for a ride out. We would usually spend the evening in Great Yarmouth. Mum and Dad were not drinkers and preferred a game of prize bingo and a go on the slot machines along the seafront. We would always end up having chips or a pie or a hot dog or something for supper. We would be in bed by about 10:30pm so that we could rise early in order to go fishing.

Dad and me on the Broads 1960

Me and my Dad Norfolk Broads 1961

The first two days, my Dad fished a certain spot on Martham Broad but kept baiting up another spot further along and less accessible, with stewed wheat and ground bait. On the third day, he told Grandad and me that he was going to fish the "awkward spot." His jaw dropped when we arrived at 5:00am because his spot was already taken, not by an angler but by a pair of swans with signets. It took ages to gently coax them into the water, but eventually, they swam off in a huff. Grandad and I fished our usual spots and did quite well with good catches of bream, but Dad had a Bream bonanza catching over 100 pounds weight of Bream between two-and-a-half pounds and seven pounds. His arms ached from playing with the fish, but as Grandad whispered to me, his arms didn't ache enough to wipe the smile off his face.

I relax for a while with my Paternal Grandparents, Lil and Walt, on Holiday in Norfolk.

Welford Reservoir

Another reservoir we spent time at was Welford Reservoir. It was quite a long walk through a wooded area, from the car park to the water, especially carrying a fishing kit. However, it was worth it just for the view and the wildlife there. We were quietly making our way along the narrow track when I almost fell over two young badgers which had been play-fighting there. They ran off when they realized we were there. I took care whenever I was near that spot, and I saw them occasionally after that. I love badgers.

There was plenty of wildlife to enjoy there. There was a field on the opposite bank, which rose up at an angle and gave such a good view. We regularly spotted rabbits and brown hares, fieldfares, a kestrel, and best of all, if we were there just as it began to get light or in the evening twilight, we sometimes watched a barn owl quartering the field for mice and field voles. As for birds on the water, we saw all sorts of waders, ducks, and waterfowl. My favourite of these was the Great Crested Grebes. They are gorgeous to look at and fascinating to watch their courtship dance ritual. Nice to see the babies riding on Mummy's back too. Dad and I had a great deal of enjoyment watching them.

My heaviest fish there was a seven-pound bream caught on bread flake. I took my mate Don there once, and just as the first rays of sunlight blessed us, a skein of Brent Geese flew overhead in vee formation against the light. Don said that it had been worth rising early and paying for the day ticket already before we had even begun fishing. On the same day, after carefully placing a half-pound Roach into his keepnet, he loudly exclaimed, "Wait till I tell the missus. A thirty-eight-pound Roach." That made us all Laugh. Roach do not grow anywhere that size. The British Record at that time was a little over four pounds.

A male Great Crested Grebe Feeds babies sitting on a nesting female's back.

CHAPTER SEVEN: JUNIOR SCHOOL

Some of the bravado that I had experienced at the end of my time at infant school had strangely evaporated after six weeks of summer holidays. A rather nervous Dennis Perkins went up to Burbage Grove Road Junior School. It was a shaky start. As I write this, sixty years later, a new Junior school has been built further along Grove Road on the opposite side and towards the church. My old Junior School is now an infant school replacing the demolished St. Catherine's Infant School, which I had attended.

Headmasters

The Headmaster, then, was a Welshman by the name of Mr. Evans. He was a jolly, kindly old soul, given to holding kids' faces in both of his hands and making their cheeks bulge by gently pulling them forward so they resembled hamsters with their cheek pouches full of stored food. He drove a beautiful two-tone Austin Cambridge A55. He retired when I was in my second year and returned to Wales and was replaced by a bloke by the name of Sherwood.

Teachers

My first teacher at Grove Road Junior was Mrs. Wright, who was a really nice lady, but after one term, she moved to another school, and for the first time, I had a man teacher. He was a tall man teacher, and I wondered if he would be a hard man. I needn't have worried. Mr. Briggs and I got on very well, and he inspired me to work harder. I actually wanted to please him, and my performance improved. Our objectives at this time were to gradually learn all of our times-tables twos up to twelves. We were also expected to improve our reading. In addition, we were introduced to history and geography.

My next teacher was Mrs. Wykes. She was the mother of one of my friends, Tim Wykes. His ironic nickname at school was "Slick" (because he wasn't slick). His Dad ran a fruit and vegetable wholesale business with quite a few lorries. They were a nice family with a good sense of humor, and Mr. Wykes was tickled pink when I told him of his son's nickname and teased Tim mercilessly, although in a humorous fashion. When he came home from work, he would loudly call "Yoo-hoo" to everyone, then "Oh look, it's our Slick, hello, son."

Mrs. Wykes was responsible for introducing me to a set of six books called the "R" mysteries by Enid Blyton. They were similar to her Famous Five books but better, in my opinion. All their titles began with the letter "R." They were:

The Rockingdown Mystery

The Rilloby Fair Mystery

The Ring 'o' Bells Mystery

The Rubadub Mystery

The Rat-a-tat Mystery

The Ragamuffin Mystery.

I loved them and read them over and over and over again. At birthdays and at Christmas, I always asked for one of these books by a specific title or a book token so I could pop into Lawrence's bookshop in Castle Street and get the book myself. I could spend hours there. Thus, I managed to accrue the full set, which I still have in my collection as I write this some sixty years later. My love of books which was to last my whole lifetime was now well and truly established.

However, I was no swot, and I was no angel. I played truant a number of times, usually with my mate Eddie. Now Eddie was no academic. He couldn't even speak English properly. He once earnestly informed me that "You should have comeded [cumdid] to my bonfire Den" We got on well enough, but I'm afraid he was a bad influence on me, and I'm ashamed to say that I acted as look-out while he broke into a house. In fact, I did it twice before coming to my senses. Another time we both decided to go to London and set off walking, following the railway track that we thought would lead us there. We got about four miles away, as far as Elmesthorpe Station [yes, Elmesthorpe did have a station in those days], before we lost our nerve and decided to return. We arrived home at about 8:00 pm. It was winter, and the night was dark. My Dad gave me a good hiding. Eddie befriended a lad who did not live in Woodland Avenue or Banky Meadow, whom I did not like at all. I stopped hanging around with Eddie. He died in his 20's in a motorbike accident.

As I moved up a class at Grove Road Junior School, I was chuffed to learn that my teacher was to be the inspirational Mr. Briggs. With his enthusiasm and positive encouragement, I continued to do well with English and even improved my arithmetic. He chose me to play the part of Joseph in the nativity play that year, and my shyness meant that I was scared stiff because not only were we to perform in front of the whole school as well as parents, but I was also required to put a guiding arm around the waist of a certain Rachael Mackey who was a girl, for goodness' sake. Don't get me wrong now, Rachael was lovely, but I couldn't be doing with girls at that age. They made my face and ears go red. However, by the time we had rehearsed and rehearsed and rehearsed again, I managed to get through it, and it went well. I even got to like Rachael in a guarded and platonic matey kind of way, of course. Looking back now, I wonder what the hell was wrong with me. She was beautiful.

Generally, I was scared of girls but grew in confidence once I got to know them. My first female friend, apart from my neighbour Dawn, was Susan, a blue-eyed blond. Then came Lynn, a dark-eyed beauty who must have really liked me because she kept giving me sweets and chocolate. I never complained. Then there was Judith. We would walk to school and back together, and she was such good company. She was so likable, funny, spirited, but down to earth. I thought she was wonderful. She had long hair, which she usually wore in two long plaits with ribbons. She lived in Woodland Avenue with her parents, two brothers, and three sisters. I knew and liked them all. Judith grew up to become involved in politics and fought tooth and nail for people who needed help. She became Mayor of Hinckley and Bosworth for a year in 1997. Sadly, she was diagnosed with cancer and put up a very brave fight for a long time but tragically died in 2010, just two weeks short of her 60th birthday. Her gravestone is near my father's grave in Hinckley cemetery, so I still occasionally stop to pay my respects to her and stand quietly for a moment in memory of those happy days from long, long ago.

The Growler

I have mixed feelings about my final year at Grove Road Juniors. It began badly with a new teacher coming to the school. Another Welshman but nothing like the old retired Headmaster, Mr. Evans. We nicknamed him the growler. He was not a nasty man in any way. I just could not get on his wavelength. There was a personality clash between us. Furthermore, things kept going wrong for me. Several times he blamed me for things I had not done. He was always growling and chuntering at me. On the first day, he was marking the register and, for some reason, put his fountain pen sideways between his teeth because he needed both hands to shuffle the pages of the large register around to find the correct page. When the register had been called, he lifted his head to address us and his tongue, lips and teeth were blue. YUK. It was horrible. We were all too scared to tell him, so he stayed like it all morning. When he returned after the lunch break, it was gone.

My work was never good enough for him. Every time I submitted some work, he growled at me, so I just gave up. On top of all that, he stripped me of my job as a milk monitor, which I really enjoyed. Two of us had to knock on every classroom door and ask each teacher how many pupils were on the register that day. This was all jotted down and totalled up, and the note was left for the milkman who delivered the regulation third of a pint, bottles in crates. Just before morning break, we sorted the correct number of bottles for each class into a crate and, using a trolley, delivered them to the appropriate classroom. Another two monitors would then collect the empties and stack them ready for the milkman the next day. I really enjoyed this job and resented the Growler, who had taken it off me for no real specific reason. My performance and my behaviour deteriorated.

Halfway through the final term, the joy of joys for me, the Growler, left the school. I neither knew nor cared why. Our new teacher was called Mr. Meakin, and he was funny, lively, enthusiastic and interesting. He knew how to bring the most humdrum lesson to life and make it enjoyable. One day, using a primus stove, he heated a little water in a Gallon can. Just as it was boiling dry, he quickly jammed on a cork a plunged the can into a huge barrel of cold water. **BANG!** The gallon can imploded and crumpled inwards. I was so impressed. So were the other lads. Not so much the girls who had all physically jumped about a foot in the air.

After that, I was in absolute awe of Mr. Meakin. My performance improved during the second half of my last year there, but the damage had been done. I just did not know the things I should have known to give me a good start at my next school which was Hastings High School in Burbage. We were to enter a streaming system. Each year at Hastings High School was streamed ALPHA, A, B, C, D, E,

F according to your learning capability assessment and preceded by the year number. Given that the C stream was average capability, I was disappointed and a bit ashamed upon hearing the news that when I attended Hastings High School, largely due to my lack of effort under the growler at Grove Road School, I was to enter the system in class 1D. I felt a bit of a failure and was rather upset for a while, but I knew full well that I only had myself to blame

Sport

We had a sports ground, and every year, we held a sports day. Mr. Briggs had noticed that I had a good "bounce" during PE lessons as I jumped up and down on the spot to warm up. He encouraged me to enter the high jump. In those years before the "Fosbury Flop" became the accepted technique in the late 1960s, we employed the scissor jump technique to try and clear the bar. Anyway, I came second in my year and enjoyed it. In my second year at Burbage Grove Road Junior School, I landed awkwardly during high jump practice and badly sprained my ankle. Disappointingly, I could not recover in time for sports day. In the third year, I came second in my year again.

I also had a little success with playing football. We played football in the street outside our prefab. There was little traffic, and that was slow, so it was quite safe. Sometimes we went up the reccy and used pullovers for goalposts. Football positions in those days were fixed at five – three – two, and in school games, I usually played as a right-back, but one day, I surged forward and scored a goal. The next day it was announced that we had been challenged to a football match by another school. I cannot remember which one. To my surprise, once all the obvious players were picked. My one and only goal were remembered, and I was picked to play the last man on the team. After that, I played a defensive role for the school team on a number of occasions, although I wasn't always picked.

In comparison to football, I never did take to cricket and often got shouted at by other keener kids for missing an easy catch because I was in a daydream, often watching birds in the nearby trees and not paying attention. I was so bored my eyes would glaze over. I would yawn and go into a trance quite quickly.

Swimming

I began to attend swimming lessons at the old Hinckley Baths on Station Road, where the public toilets are now. A local legend by the name of Mr. Ellis [Ted] was the Manager of the baths and also the swimming instructor. He was responsible for teaching thousands of kids from Hinckley and the surrounding villages to swim during his long service. He was a funny and likable man but stood no nonsense. He taught me well. I was a strong, confident swimmer, and I worked my way through my swimming Grades before starting lessons in lifesaving techniques on Friday evenings. I was basically taught several different methods of retrieving a person in difficulty from the water. The method used depended upon the circumstances. I'm sure these methods would be well out of date now.

The other part of the lesson was how to get someone who was full of water to start breathing again. This included artificial respiration. After a while, a new technique called mouth-to-mouth resuscitation or the kiss of life was utilised. For some reason, these lessons were only run during the winter. I attained 3 Life Saving Standards. After the lessons, we would emerge from the swimming baths into the cold air and head straight for Banners café, which was located at the end of the Regent Street Arcade opposite the Regent cinema. I would order a sausage cob with Flag fruity brown sauce and a mug of steaming hot frothy Horlicks. This was bliss, especially on a cold winter night.

With Mr. Ellis's encouragement, I began a training program for long-distance swimming. I would swim 72 lengths of the old baths [one mile] front breaststroke two or three times a week. In swimming, as in the running, I was useless at short-distance sprinting, but I had stamina and was able to just keep going. After training and breaking through the aching limbs phase, I felt I could go on forever and increased my swims to 108 lengths [one and a half miles]. At least one swim a week would be on my back [crawl], starting at 36 lengths [half a mile], then up to 72, then 108 lengths.

This activity developed over a few years until I got involved in long-distance swimming for charity. I regularly swam down rivers and across lakes with a couple of other swimmers, sometimes three or four. It was always properly organized with a safety boat and stewards and so on. I seriously, really do believe, at that point in time, that I could have breast-stroked my way across the channel to France. There was some talk of trying to obtain sponsorship for me, but it just didn't materialize.

Holidays

I had become a policeman, and I was driving my police car and ringing the bell for all I was worth. [emergency service vehicles did not have sirens in those days] I was traveling really fast, chasing some robbers, but frustratingly, although I was trying to steer a straight line, somehow I was going around in circles. That's the only trouble with kids' merry-go-rounds.

The Seaside

One day when I was only three, my Dad, who cycled to work in those days, came home driving a big old grey van with Dad's bike in the back. He had borrowed the van from a kind workmate, and the next day, I was woken up very early, and after a drink and a bowl of cereals, I was taken out to the van. After some hustle and bustle, we set off on our first family holiday. I have no idea where we went. I knew we were going to 'the seaside.' I had no idea at that tender age that there was more than one seaside. We had little money but had a great time on the beach making sandcastles and playing football and cricket. We walked a lot too. I did enjoy a couple of rides on that little merry-go-round.

All three of us slept in the back of the van for two nights. We had found a quiet spot to park. Each morning I went with my Dad into the public toilets for a wash and brushed up, costing tuppence [two old pence]. The attendant was a cheerful, talkative old chap, and he let me go in for a wash with Dad for no extra charge. Mum, of course, went into the ladies to ablute. On both mornings, we entered a white-painted wooden shack on the promenade for breakfast. I shared a mug of tea with Mum and enjoyed a small bowl of beans and a slice of toast, while my parents preferred a bacon sandwich. On both days we ate a good roast dinner in a 'cheap and cheerful café. In the evenings, we would walk along the seafront and enjoy our supper, which was chips, eaten from a newspaper on a bench.

All too soon, our little shoestring holiday was over, and we returned to Hinckley, and the van went back to its generous owner. I daresay my parents had wished for something better, but I loved that holiday, and we talked about it for ages. It really set us off on enjoying our holidays.

Cliftonville

This was our first proper holiday, really. Mum had been saving very hard for us to go to Cliftonville down in Kent. I was only four years old, but I clearly remember arriving at the Castle Street corner with the Lawns near the Castle Tavern, waiting to board the old red and white coach with the single-seat driver's cab. My Dad stood a large suitcase upright and told me to sit on it, leaning my back against the Castle Tavern wall. I was told emphatically NOT to move. There were other coaches nearby and lots of people. It was very busy as over a hundred passengers waited to hand their luggage to the driver for loading before boarding their respective vehicles. Several local service buses stopped to drop off and pick up passengers at the Lawns bus stop, and the occasional taxi dropped people off and added to the general hustle and bustle. I obeyed my Dad and sat still, feeling very excited and taking in the scene.

All at once, we suddenly found ourselves sitting in the coach along with my Auntie Anne, who was eleven years old at the time and our neighbours, the Jameson family. What a journey that was. An old coach, [even then] which was by no means a luxury coach, very slowly made it s way down to Kent. There were no motorways in those days and no by-passes. We chugged slowly through towns and cities, clocking about 180 miles. It took most of the day. However, eventually, we made it to Cliftonville. We immediately looked for the sea, and I almost cried when I failed to find it. The tide goes out for miles at Cliftonville. We were all shattered by our journey and were glad to find our Guest House and enjoy an evening meal. We managed a short walk along the seafront, and I was much happier once I had actually seen the sea. [the tide had come in] We collapsed in our comfortable beds for a good night's sleep. We were lucky with the weather that week and had a lovely time in the sunshine playing on the beach every day.

Hastings

The following year we did it all again, but this time, we only took my Aunt Anne with us, and instead of traveling in a coach, Dad drove us down there in his 'new' fifteen-year-old Ford Ten car named Ada. We stayed in a really nice guest house run by a lovely lady called Mrs. Goldsborough. The food was lovely. Again the weather was good, and again we had a great time playing on the beach.

Mablethorpe

It was later in the year when we decided to have a weekend at Mablethorpe. We had a nice time [we always did], and on the return journey, we stopped for something to eat. After we had devoured the chips we bought and quenched our thirst with orange squash, we set off, but as we did so, the clutch went. "Oh no!" exclaimed Dad, "Ada's conked out." Dad managed to get us to a garage, but it was closed. The owner was just locking up. He explained that he had no mechanics around to help but, after making a telephone call, arranged for a garage further down the road to fix it for us. We had been told to ask a man called 'Bandit' who had promised on the telephone to try and help us. It's not easy to drive a car when you cannot change gears, but Dad managed to get us safely about five miles down the road stuck in second gear. We found the garage and asked the man at the desk if Bandit was around. He was summoned, and we immediately realized why he had gained the nickname of Bandit. He only had one arm. We were rather taken aback to think that this poor man was going to mend our car with only one arm. I mean, how do you even screw a nut and bolt together with only one arm? Can this really be? We wondered. Indeed it was to be, and indeed, he did mend it. We were grateful to him and absolutely in awe of his skill. We arrived home a bit late but safe, sound, amazed and, yes, humbled.

Get Yarmouth

I would have been about seven years old when we first decided to spend our summer holiday in Great Yarmouth. Mum booked us into a guest house on Wellesley Road. We had a lovely time, and being a little better placed financially this year, we had a ride out on some days and got to know the area a bit. We visited the broads a few times, and Dad got to weigh up the fishing for future reference. We also dropped into several little places North of Great Yarmouth again for future reference regarding holidays. Mum and Dad enjoyed the odd game of prize Bingo on the seafront. I enjoyed the large peddle racing cars near Wellington Pier. We were also able to book ourselves in for a performance at the circus and also a show on Britannia Pier starring Des 'o' Connor with Jack Douglas. We were beginning to expand our holiday activities.

There followed about another eight years of us taking holidays in Great Yarmouth and the surrounding area. We often had family members with us. I remember staying in a wonderful old house that had been divided up into self-catering holiday flats. There was a lovely walled-off garden complete with a huge live tortoise. Whenever we returned to our flats after being out, we used to say, "Let's find Toby. [our own name for the tortoise.] We stayed there with my Gran and Grandad Perkins and Gran's sister Edna and her husband, Harry.

We then began to stay in caravans. There were numerous sites along the coast from Great Yarmouth, Northwards at Caister-on-Sea, California, Scratby and Hemsby. We enjoyed staying in caravans so much that in 1961 my parents scrimped and saved for their own caravan. It was very old and made of painted hardboard instead of metal, but it was waterproof. Dad sited it at the Wild Duck caravan site just outside of Belton, some ten miles approximately South West of Great Yarmouth. He sold it for next to nothing a few years later, and we then enjoyed several holidays at Caister-on-Sea Holiday Camp.

Me and Dad having fun on the four-wheeler

Young me at Gt Yarmouth

My Aunt Anne and I on holiday

CHAPTER EIGHT: MUSIC

I have always liked music. I enjoy a wide range of different types of music. I never saw the point of just being fanatical about one music genre. Each to his own, of course, but I prefer to enjoy a wide range of music, so my considerable music collection on vinyl, cassettes and compact discs contain all sorts of stuff. It began with Michael Holiday, then stuff from the 1950s charts such as Buddy Holly, Eddie Cochrane, Nat King Cole, Perry Como, Rosemary Clooney, Elvis Presley, Guy Mitchell, Sam Cooke, The Everly Brothers, The Platters, Pat Boone, Andy Williams, Chuck Berry and many more.

In the early 1960's we moved on to the likes of Lonnie Donegan, Anthony Newly, The Shadows, The Tornados, Del Shannon, Helen Shapiro, Eden Kane, and Shirley Bassey. Then, beginning in 1963, the biggest phenomenon that the music industry had ever experienced occurred when the Fab Four from Liverpool burst onto the pop scene to be not only mega-popular but also a massive influence on other musicians and songwriters. They were quickly joined by a massive emergence of singers and beat groups to make the 1960's one of the most exciting musical experiences of all time. The Beatles changed everything and completely blew me away.

I disagree with the commonly held opinion that says you can't like the Beatles and the Stones, so you must like one or the other. I say RUBBISH. This is what I call 'The US and THEM syndrome, sufferers of which have a strong need and have to have someone to rail against, someone to love and someone to hate. I love both the Beatles and the Stones. Whilst we are on the subject of common beliefs, there are those who say that if you can remember the sixties, you weren't there. What TRIPE. There are plenty of us who had a fantastic time in the sixties, thank you, without the need for mind altering substances. We weren't all mindless junkies. The music of the sixties was new and exciting, and I loved it, but equally, I can enjoy a brass band or folk music or a bit of classical. Mozart, in particular. Don't get me wrong, though. I don't enjoy everything. I don't care for rapping, for instance.

I was very lucky that in the early 1960s, my Dad bought a radiogram. It had a huge speaker and a lovely tone. We bought a single vinyl 45rpm record every week. My Mum and Dad chose the first few records before [to their great credit] recognized my massive enthusiasm and let me choose every other week. Music was becoming ever more important to me at this time. My main love was the Beatles, and soon I was saving for their albums or LP's [Long Play] as we called them, and with the help of birthday monies and a few small loans, I managed to buy every record they ever released as they released them. By the time they released their Album 'Beatles for Sale' they had all but conquered America, and Beatlemania had swept the world. There followed a tide of new bands, predominantly from Liverpool [the Merseybeat Sound] and from Manchester, but other places too. The Rolling Stones, Gerry and the Pacemakers, the Hollies, The Who, Billy J Krama and the Dakotas, Freddie and the Dreamers, the Searchers, the Dave Clarke Five, the Moody Blues, Spencer Davis, the Lovin Spoonful, Sonny and Cher, the Troggs, the Beachboys, the Yardbirds, Herman's Hermits, the Animals, Manfred Mann, Peter and Gordon, Wayne Fontana and the mind-benders, the Kinks and many, many more.

Solo singers were still doing well during this period, even ballad singers. Jim Reeves, Andy Williams, Aretha Franklin, Shirley Bassey, Dusty Springfield, Dionne Warwick, Brenda Lee Cilla Black, Sandy Shaw and Barbra Streisand, to name but a few. Hardly a single day went by when we didn't have a new single to listen to. There were several TV pop music programmes, Oh Boy, Six-Five Special, Jukebox Jury, etc., but the most influential was 'Top of the Pops. Pirate Radios blasted this music out twenty-four hours a day, every day, followed by the emergence of Radio One. The DJs felt like they were friends introducing us to new sounds so quickly that it was a job to keep up with it all. We were bombarded, and we loved it.

I still have my extensive 45 rpm single collection from this time, along with a fair number of vinyl albums. I found it such a pleasure to go into my favourite music shop [Russells in Castle Street, Hinckley], Flip through the 45s or LPs, listen to a couple in the sound-proof booths and finally make my choice. In time we went on to cassette tapes and then CDs. Some of us, [but not me], went onto digital downloads. They can do want they want and play it how they like, but nobody will convince me that the quantity and quality and innovation and talent that gushed into our lives like a high-power water hose during the 1960s had anything anywhere near approaching comparison to it either before or since.

That isn't to say that there wasn't good music before and since, but nothing to have such an effect on a whole generation of young people who, looking back, were so privileged to be targeted by such a barrage of new and exciting sounds and artists. There was a youth club at the rear of Hinckley College of Further Education approached from Bowling Green Road. Every week a crowd of local teenagers squeezed in to listen to a great DJ who played us the latest music and pop videos. I had a great time every Tuesday with my mates, drinking coke, chatting the girls up and absorbing the music. Later in 1967, I sat in the Junction and watched a worldwide video on a huge screen.
It was the Beatles 'All you need is Love' It just blew me away. It's in the top ten magic memories of my life.

CHAPTER NINE: THE SCOUT MOVEMENT

The Scout Promise (at the time that I was in the Scouts)

On my honour, I promise that I will do my best,

To do my duty to God and the Queen,

To help other people at all times, To obey the Scout Law.

The Scout Law (at that time)

1. *A Scout's honour is to be trusted.*
2. *A Scout is Loyal to the Queen, his Country, his Scouters, his Parents, his Employers and those under him.*
3. *A Scout's duty is to be useful and to help others.*
4. *A Scout is a friend to all and a brother to every other scout, no matter what country, class or creed the other may belong*
5. *A Scout is Courteous.*
6. *A Scout is a friend to animals.*
7. *A Scout obeys orders of his parents, patrol leader or scoutmaster without question.*
8. *A Scout smiles and whistles under all difficulties.*
9. *A Scout is thrifty.*
10. *A Scout is clean in thought, word and deed.*

The Promise and the Law had to be learned by heart and recited by new scouts when they were invested. Only at that point is a Wolf Cub entitled to wear the troop neckerchief with a woggle.

Wolf Cubs

When I first joined Cubs in 1958, the 1st Burbage Scout Group utilized a large old wooden hut for their headquarters. It was located about a mile away from our prefab home near the centre of old Burbage. To get there, we turned off Windsor Street into Ball's Lane [now called Britannia Road] along the side of the old barracks. We then had to walk along a footpath over some waste ground near where the Millennium Hall car park is today. This brought us out straight onto a large area containing playing fields. It was called the Old Boys Rec. [recreation ground], named after the football team Burbage Old Boys, whose home ground it was. The 1st Burbage Scout Hut was the first hut, and Burbage Old Boys had the second wooden hut, which was used as a changing room. There was no outside lighting across the wasteland, so we all carried torches in the winter months. It was black as pitch, and you could easily injure yourself by stumbling on the rough terrain.

I was welcomed by a lovely lady called Jean Lovett, who was the Cub leader and was called by her Cub name of, Akela [The Indian Wolf]. She had a number of helpers, the main one of which was a lady whose real name is lost in the mists of time, but her Cub name was Bagheera [The Black Panther]. The Wolf Cub pack was split into sixes. I was to be adopted by the Blue Six. There was the Red Six and Gold Six etc. Each Six had a leader called a Sixer, and each Sixer had an assistant called a Seconder.

Wolf cub pack meetings were a mixture of official stuff such as an inspection to see how well we were turned out, breaking the flag, investiture of newly joined cubs, working towards earning various badges and receiving notices of forthcoming activities and camps etc. The rest of the time was spent playing organized games. Some were very physical, whilst others were designed to get your brain cells working. After the meeting, my Dad and our next-door neighbour would take turns to collect Ian and me from the chip shop around the corner from the Scout hut for which we were made an allowance from our respective parents, usually enough for chips and sausage or fishcake and of course we would always ask the chip shop server politely if we could have batter bits on our chips. In other parts of the UK, these are known as scratchings or simply scraps.

There were often 'district' cub activities and, in particular, sports days. I wasn't particularly sporty. I did fairly well in the high jump and triple jump, and I could swim like a fish. I was a reasonable long-distance runner and a good long-distance swimmer. I did have stamina but wasn't good at short sprints on land or in the water.

The trouble was that I barely raised a zero on my personal competitive scale. Other kids would say to me, "My Dad is bigger than your Dad," and I would reply, "Yes, he is," which would kill the conversation stone dead and avoid the usual, tiresome, relentless arguments that most other kids got involved in on a daily basis. Another was, "I can run faster than you, Perkins" I would retort, "Off you go then." I cared, not a jot either way.

District Cubs Annual Sports Day

I remember one particular district cub sports day. It was held at Mount Grace High school in Butt Lane Hinckley. I hadn't bothered to enter any events but asked my Dad if he would drop me off and pick me up so I could watch. He decided to stay and watch with me. I'm in no doubt that he thought he was being supportive, but I knew there would be trouble. "Have you entered the high jump?" he asked.

"No, Dad"

"Why not? You could win it, you know."

“Didn’t want to.”

“Have you entered for the triple jump, then?”

“No.”

“Well, what events have you entered then?

“None”

“NONE? Why on earth not.”

“Don’t want to Dad,”

“Don’t be silly. Go down to the Official's Tent now and enter something.”

“Don’t want to.”

He was irritated and obviously disappointed, but I just wasn’t interested. I couldn’t understand why he was so wound up about it. After all, I hadn’t even asked him to come. I had merely asked for transport to and from.

After watching a few events, I asked him if I could have an ice cream from the van parked in the corner of the field.

“No! But if you enter an event, I’ll buy you an ice cream afterward.”

“Okay then.”

“Okay, what? You’ll enter an event?”

“No, I’ll go without.”

He was absolutely exasperated with me and could not hide his disappointment and irritation.

A while later, Jean Lovett, our Akela, spoke to me. "Dennis" she called as she approached me. "Can I ask you to enter the 440yds, please? We have no one entered. Most of our best runners have done several events each and are worn out. We must have an entry, or 1st Burbage will be the laughing stock. Can I put you down for it?..... Please."

"Yes, of course," To me, this was different. I had been put on the spot and could help with a specific issue. I didn't want to let the side down, and besides, I really liked our Akela.

My Dad shook his head as I began to warm up. No doubt he was wondering why I did it for Akela but not for him. He just didn't get it. However, he cheered up a bit and gave me a pep talk about the run. I gave it my best shot.

From the start, six runners accelerated up the track. The winner crossed the finish line about twenty yards in front of everyone else. One guy was lagging about as far behind, and four of us crossed the line almost together. I was surprised when my name was shouted as the official announced that I had come SECOND. Akela thanked me. My mates slapped my back and yelled, "Well Done," and my Dad was cock-a-hoop. "I told you, didn't I?" he said. What hokey do you want? [hokey is a local term for ice cream]. Dad was as good as his word.

Weekend camps were held at Fox Coverts, on woodland owned by the district scouting commission, some 8 miles away near Kirkby Mallory. I loved camping which again was a mixture of education, tasks, exercise and games. The only jarring aspect of this was that I was the new kid and turned up to my first camp with my kit in a suitcase because my parents could not afford to buy me a traditional camping rucksack just at that particular time. Everyone else had rucksacks or kitbags, and some of the older cubs openly criticized me for it. At that time, people were still obsessed with the class system, and there were also snobbish, sly remarks about me living in a prefab due to my shyness, my face burned red, and there were times I wished that I wasn't there. However, I stuck it out, and so it was that I enjoyed my three years with 1st Burbage Wolf Cubs, a sort of ongoing boot camp to prepare us for the Boy Scouts. I learned a lot, enjoyed some good times and made some friends. I eventually became a Sixer of the Blue six for a few months before leaving to move up to the Boy Scouts. I took part in lots of marches and parades for St. George's Day etc.

Fire

In the early 1960s, there was a fire that destroyed not only our scout hut but most of our camping equipment and a homemade pedal-powered go-cart that we had made and entered into the annual Scouting Organisation's National competition. Given that we only had a few weeks to go before the competition, we struggled. However, the 4th Hinckley Group were good to us, letting us use their hut on days and evenings that they did not use it. We made another Go-Cart just in time, but on that day, we were disqualified because the brakes did not meet the specified requirements. When the commentator explained our situation over the public address system, we got a huge cheer and a prolonged round of applause.

Our new scout hut was erected fairly quickly. A local builder laid a concrete base with drainage etc., for the cost price of materials, and we were offered two prefabs [very similar to the one I lived in] from a site in Leicester where they were dismantling them and scrapping them. Another local company supplied transport to collect the insulation boards, and I, along with two other scouts, Dave Callow and Dean Hay, volunteered to help load and unload this huge lorry. I believe the camping equipment was insured, so we were operating as normal fairly quickly.

The Friday evening meetings ran a similar course to the Cubs meetings. They were a mixture of official stuff. Practicing or learning things like knot tying, campfire cooking, bird and tree type recognition, and clothes repair (sewing, etc.) to earn badges. There were loads of them, so during my time at the Boy Scouts, I learned a lot about how to be independent and how to look after myself, how to keep myself clean and healthy, how to find or build a shelter in the outdoors and how to feed myself, how to make calls from the old red telephone boxes, including reverse charge calls. [before mobile phones were invented] etc. My trouble was that I was a somewhat belligerent teenager and often did not respect people as much as I should have done. Just a few years after that, I came to intensely regret my previous attitude and bad behaviour. Eventually, I grew out of my arrogant teenage ways, but disappointingly, it was often too late to build bridges with some good people who deserved better from me.

Scouting People

Upon attending my first meeting, I was initially a little confused. There were no less than three Kens amongst the adult helpers/leaders known collectively as Scouters. There was Ken Reece, who was the official Scoutmaster. Then there was Ken Wainwright, who was Scout Master over the Senior Scouts who were aged 14 plus. Ken Wainwright also helped out. Generally, the cubs and scouts called him Skip, but the Scouters and parents called him Ken. The third Ken was Ken Bell, who was an Assistant Scoutmaster.

All three "Kens" had been Scouts themselves in their younger days and had gone on to become Scout Masters (SM) or Assistant Scout Masters (ASM). The people who looked after and organised Scouts were generally called Scouters.

Incidentally, even in those days of the 1960s, they had to be vetted and qualified. As time went on, Ken Bell disappeared and, if I remember rightly, suffered a long illness of some sort.

Scout groups are often associated with churches and chapels, and Ken Reece appears to have moved from the 10th Hinckley Congregational Group to set up the 1st Burbage Group associated in the early days with Burbage Congregational Church.
Other Scouters joined us to lend a hand. The local bobby [who knew me well, as our paths had already crossed] was hard but fair, and in spite of the odd clout metered out by him, I liked and respected him. [It wasn't unusual to receive a light cuff from a policeman in those days for, say, riding a bike with no lights or riding on the pavement or being cheeky or scrumping fruit] He was a big man, but he would never, ever hit kids with any real force but just enough, a sharp reminder, to help you to understand that he was the boss. He never cuffed anyone in his capacity as Assistant Scoutmaster
(ASM) either. He wasn't a bully. It was just the way it was at that time.

The next ASM to join us came to live in our area from another part of the country when I was about 13, and quite honestly, I was becoming a bit of a challenging handful. I had become a bit of a rebel. He, too, was a policeman. I wasn't so keen on him. He was hard and strict, and we clashed quite a lot. I remember his young child, a toddler, who died in a fishpond drowning accident, and of course, I was really sorry for that and felt sad for him.

The last ASM I remember joining us was a young feller by the name of Mick Varden. He had started off with the 1st Burbage as a cub, grown up with the Boy Scouts and then Senior Scouts [14 years onwards] and then qualified as an ASM. He was about 18 years old and very much in touch with us because he was nearer our age.
He and I shared a love of the Beatles' music and had many conversations about the Beatles and music in general. Other helpers I remember were Colin Sheriff and Ex-Scouts, Anthony Dixon and Michael Hunter.

Ken Reece – Scoutmaster

Although I did not always realize it at the time, Ken Reece was brilliant at what he did and taught me so much incredible stuff even though I was sometimes badly behaved. Ken Reece was of average build with short hair and always looked smart. He ran a plumbing business, and even in his working clothes, he always managed to make me look down at myself and feel scruffy. When camping, Ken Reece was an absolute top man at the organisation.

1. Details of the camp, including dates, address and costs, were issued to parents months in advance. A telephone number was listed for questions or any special dietary needs etc.

2. A list of clothing and equipment was issued at the same time. Best scout uniform for out-of-camp activities only. The second pair of shorts, shirt and plimsolls (no socks) were used for the entire camp. One old jersey, one pair of black boots, and one pair of plimsolls. Wash kit, shoeshine kit, torch, eating utensils, 2 plates, and 1 mug, all marked for I/d. Any clothes or kit over and above the issued list would be confiscated and stored and then returned as we packed to leave for home on the last day.

3. An account at the "Camp Bank" was opened for each scout. This enabled parents to save weekly for the cost of the camp, and there was a modest MAXIMUM spending money added. Scouts were not directly in charge of their own money. They were issued with blank printed cheques, which they had to fill in to draw cash or spend at the camp tuckshop. These could then be approved or not if the spend was too big to leave a suitable amount in for the days left or if the purchase was not sensible. Ken Reece himself had the final say.

4. Transport to camp was arranged and announced nearer the time with details of where parents could drop off their little darlings and, again, a contact number supplied for any worries or questions.

5. The camp was insured for accidents, and details were passed to parents.

6. A parents' camp visit day and details were issued.

7. We occasionally had the luxury of coach travel, but more often than not, a huge box-type truck was hired by a driver from a local transport company. We all helped to load tents and equipment onto the lorry before including our own. We then piled in ourselves, arranging makeshift seats for ourselves among the equipment. I don't suppose it would be allowed nowadays, but it worked very well for us, particularly as regular comfort breaks were made en route.

8. Upon arrival at the Worldwide Scouting Organisation-approved campsite, we were allowed 15 minutes to stretch our legs. Then at Ken Reece's signal, we unloaded our own rucksack. These were placed in one huge pile well away from the central area of the campsite. With that done, again, under instruction, we off-loaded all the equipment and placed it in the locations indicated. There would be 8 berth Icelandic ridge tents, one for each patrol, which also had a grub tent to store supplies and equipment. [I was in the Otters], Scouters slept in 2 Berth Tents. There were two toilet tents containing chemical toilets and a Scouter Tent for their day-to-day requirements. Corrugated zinc sheets and iron grids for making alter fires, Water carriers, tea chests containing axes, bowsaws, spades, rope, pulleys, cooking pots, pans, and utensils, washing up liquid, breakfast cereals, jam, eggs, baked beans, spuds, lard, butter first aid kits, toilet rolls, tea towels, Brillo pads, tea cloths, – you name it – it was on Ken Reece's List and therefore on the lorry.

9. Once it was all offloaded, there was a meeting for Scouters, Patrol Leaders and Seconds. Ken Reece motivated everyone and gave out

instructions. The Patrol Leaders (PL's) and Seconds delegated tasks to the rest of the scouts. We were all so busy, but it seemed that in no time at all, tents were up. Toilets were up and charged with chemicals. Personal kit was placed in the Icelandic 8's with bedrolls rolled out, ready for sleep. Cooking pots, utensils and provisions were stored in the grub tents. Each patrol built and lit an alter fire. Each patrol had dug a dry sump and a wet sump with ferns spread over. A couple of latrines had been dug out, pebbles dropped in, and ferns laid. This was for weeing only to prevent the toilets [which we called the bogs] from filling up before the end of camp. These were for pooing only. (Known as number twos) Sticks were gathered and hammered into the ground, and sisal tied along to form a sort of line fence in order to define each patrol's territory. A gateway was left for exit and entry. Each patrol sawed enough logs and gathered enough kindling to start an altar fire the next day [to cook breakfast]. This was also kept in the grub tent in case it rained at night. By the time we had done all this, the Scouters had got their fire going, and we were treated to a lovely chunky soup for supper prepared and cooked by…… yes, Ken Reece. We did not even have to wash up. The Scouters did it for us. We were absolutely knackered from the journey and the work involved in setting up the camp.

10. In the following days, tasks were allocated for breakfast, inspection and meal times. The necessary tasks were rotated each day, so by the end of the camp. Each scout had done everything. We rose fairly early, and if we didn't, a Scouter would come and liven us up to get us moving.
    Tasks were something like:-

Tasks at Camp

Two scouts would work together to get breakfast. [daily menus for each meal were kept in the grub tent [guess who devised and wrote them out? That's right – Ken Reece] One of these would be to rake out the altar fire ashes from the previous day while the other breakfast duty scout would fetch dry kindling and logs from the grub tent. While one was lighting the fire, the other would select the required breakfast ingredients and bring them to a table near the altar fire.

NB 1: The idea of an altar fire is that logs are fed in one end and, as they burn, are gently raked to the other end as embers. As with a barbecue, cooking was done over embers, but large billycans or dixies containing soups or water for washing up were placed over the flaming logs to get them going. It was rare not to have a dixie of water heating on the altar fire for washing up, and nobody would be allowed to eat unless that was the case.

NB 2: The policy with used food tins was burned, bashed and buried. Burned in the fire to soften them, bashed flat with a tent peg mallet while still warm and placed in the dry sump. This was filled with earth at the end of camp. As much waste as possible was burned. Paper, eggshells, waste food, everything except for liquid which was minimal and went in the wet sump.

Whilst the two breakfast scouts were lighting the fire and cooking breakfast afterward – the rotor for tasks came into play [you know who devised and wrote them]. More wood would be chopped or sawn but only by scouts who had achieved their axeman-ship badge. The ferns across wet sumps and latrines would be spread nearby to dry out in the sun until they could be burned on the altar fire and new ferns applied. Five-gallon jerry cans were used to fetch water, and these had to be filled. Washing up was done, and drying up followed, but it was left on a thick plastic sheet ready for inspection. The tent brailings would be un-hooked, and the walls rolled up along with the doors at each end to ensure that fresh air circulated underneath and through the tent. Sleeping bags would be hung to air on a line that ran along just under the tent ridge.

The groundsheet, twelve feet by eight feet, was dragged out into the fresh air, squared up with the wall of the tent flattened, smoothed out and left flat on the ground. Every scout had to wash, clean his teeth and, if we were going out, wear the best uniform [when all the jobs were done.] Finally, we each had to arrange our own personal kit in the space on the groundsheet that we slept in. Rucksacks at the top, clothes, eating utensils and wash-kits, with footwear at the bottom. Plimsoles if you were staying in the camp that morning or black shoes or boots if you had your best uniform on. Everything on the groundsheet had to be visible.

Daily Inspection

Every morning a Scouter would arrive to inspect the tents, groundsheet, equipment, washing up, personal kit, the site and the scouts. Rejected washed-up eating and cooking utensils would have to be done again and re-inspected. They had to be spotless. We got through tons of Brillo pads. He would mark you to a system, again devised by Ken Reece. You would also feed a different Scouter each day who would eat what you had cooked. He would often arrive early to observe activity, and again, the Patrol would be assessed and marked. However, advice was always available, and encouragement was abundant.

The inspection would start with the Inspector's command Patrol…….patrol-alert! This meant standing in line, to attention in front of the groundsheet, in your personal kit. Following the "Stand at ease" order, it began with a few questions. Is anybody feeling unwell? Has everyone had some breakfast? In the last 24 hours, has everyone been to the toilet for a Number 1?……… and Number 2?........... Is anybody worried about anything? If you want to see me after the inspection on our own, that's fine. He would then address the Patrol Leader [PL]. Has everyone behaved? Has everyone pulled their weight with tasks? The inspection would then begin in earnest. Points were totted up, and there were patrol prizes and personal prizes, which were dished out on the last day of camp.

When all this was over, we all moved over to the flagpole near the Scouter's tent. We stood in a semi-circle around the flagpole in our patrols. Ken Reece then addressed us. He started with a short prayer and would nominate someone to break the union flag. He would then impart any important information to us, comment on our performance so far, adding criticism and encouragement where he felt they were needed. Sometimes he added tips on how we could improve and always offered instruction or training if we requested it. The activities planned for that day were then outlined with Do's and Don'ts.

Sunday Church Parade

On Sunday, we always went to a local church in our best uniforms and highly polished boots. It was always the nearest Christian church, regardless of which religious denomination. Nearly all of them seemed pleased to have their congregation swelled by about 30 odd Scouters and Scouts in smart uniforms and buffed-up boots. We were often especially welcomed from the pulpit and sometimes included in their prayers. Sometimes we could not get away after the service because members of the congregation would want to talk to us and ask questions. The conversation would go on for ages. It was heart-warming.

The only church we went to where we were allowed in but otherwise totally ignored was a strict Catholic one. There were less than a dozen members of the congregation. We were kept standing throughout the service, which was completely spoken in Latin, so we did not understand a thing that was going on. We may as well not have been there. No real welcome, no contact, no mention, no connection, no warmth, and no Goodbyes even. Well, you know what you can do - Father Grumpy-old sod. We have visited far better and friendlier Catholic Churches than yours as well as other denominations.

Camps at Fox Coverts

I lost count of the times I camped for weekends at Fox Coverts. This was a large campsite with tracks, footpaths, woodland areas and about six or seven separate campsites. One for each Cub scout group in the local vicinity. There was a communal area with a large hut, flagpoles and a huge campfire area. Sometimes these weekend camps were for training purposes. Sometimes they ran special activities or competitions. Sometimes it could just be a free weekend to do as we wish. Whatever it was, you had to apply for its use to the scouting organization's District Commissioner [DC]. His name was Bill Seal. He was a maths teacher at Hinckley Grammar school. He had a reputation for being fierce and Grumpy. He was rather a formidable character but only refused your application if there was already something happening there on the dates you had applied for.

If we happened to be up and about early morning or still out as it got dark, we saw lots of wildlife at Fox Coverts. We regularly saw squirrels, foxes and badgers at quite close quarters, as well as a whole range of moles, shrews, mice and birds. I often observed a Barn Owl silently quartering a field on the other side of the plantation. Every so often, I would also catch a glimpse of a Little Owl. I often wondered how much the sounds made by owls were responsible for the scary tales of Mad Margaret's well, told and re-told by the older lads in order to scare the younger lads. These tales were often passed down through generations. Other birds were abundant too. Peewits in the nearby fields swallows near the hut. Sightings of blackbirds, thrushes, sparrows, starlings, chaffinches, robins, goldfinches, bullfinches, wood pigeons, fieldfares, blue tits, great tits, long-tailed tits and blackcaps were common occurrences. I loved them all.

If only two of us camped overnight or for a weekend and had travelled there on our bikes, we would often cycle back to Earl Shilton and visit the fish and chip shop for our evening meal. Other times we would cycle in the other direction and visit my Auntie Val, who lived in Newbold – Verdon. She would make us eggs and chips.

When I had first been made up to Patrol Leader of the Otter Patrol, I felt the need to get my patrol to Fox coverts for a weekend so that I could pass on some of my camping experience to the younger ones and try to get them working more as a team. I approached Ken Reece for permission. He was all for it. "Good Idea Mr. Perkins" he enthused. "Here's the application form. Fill it in and take it to Bill Seal at his home address on Saturday Morning. …….and by the way, go smartly dressed and call him Mr. Seal – NOT Bill." Apparently, a couple of hours on a Saturday morning were set aside for such things by the scary Mr. Bill Seal.

When the day came, I found Bill Seal's rather posh house and climbed the few steps to his front door. With some trepidation, I rang his doorbell. The door was suddenly and violently yanked open, making me jump. I was so on edge. He was quite a big chap, and as he stood two steps above me, he looked enormously tall. This also gave him a psychological advantage. "Yes?" he snapped loudly. I had to resist the temptation to turn and run away.

"Please, Sir, Mr. Seal, I have an application for a weekend Patrol Camp at Fox Coverts." He motioned to me to follow him in and sat down at a beautiful huge roll-top desk at the side of which I remained standing. "Why? When? How many? Names" Bill Seal's questions came short, sharp and quick-fire, asking for information I had already entered into the Application Form. When he was satisfied, he reached into a drawer and pulled out a stamp and ink pad. **BANG! BANG! BANG!** The stamp hit the inkpad and each copy of the form with rapid sickening crashes, which again startled me. At this rate, I thought, I would soon be a nervous wreck. There was a nominal charge of five shillings for this service and camp insurance, for which Ken Reece had given me cash from scout funds. I duly signed the form and paid up.

Bill Seal swivelled around on his office chair to face me directly. He appeared to be struggling with some inner emotion. His facial features seemed to be out of control. With a slight tilt of his head, his face contorted. His eyes were slits - almost closed. He seemed to overcome his natural urge to scowl at me. With a final super effort, he blurted out, “Have a good weekend at camp,” and shook me firmly by the left hand, a secret scouting practice in those days. As I walked back home, I just could not believe it. In fact, I was absolutely amazed, almost in shock. Bill Seal had just SMILED at me. Of course, he may just have had wind.

I would like to report that my initiative produced excellent results, but once again, things went wrong for me. There were two brothers in my patrol, Richard Maycock, the same age as me and his younger brother Geoff who was a new recruit. Geoff was, as yet, not invested. He was not allowed to wear the 1st Burbage all-green neckerchief. This was his first time away from his Mum and Dad. On the second day, Richard approached me to inform me that their younger brother Geoff was badly homesick and that he was taking him back home. I could not believe it. “What, on day two?” I protested incredulously, but Richard was adamant that they would leave and that it would not be worth him coming back as it meant a twelve-mile bike ride each way. Despite this setback, I liked the two brothers and did not want to fall out with them. “OK, then, Rich” Then there were four.

Unknown to us at the time, a couple of older scouts, almost ready to move to the Senior Scouts, crept into Fox Coverts and, unknown to us, camped in another part of the site. At nightfall, my Patrol were all sitting around an altar fire, drinking tea and chatting. David [Higgo] Higginson suddenly yelled out that he had seen someone in the woods who had immediately disappeared. This put us slightly on edge. It was a courtesy to pay a brief visit to any other scout group camping on the site so that you knew who was there. The absence of such a visit led us to believe that whoever was wandering around in the woods did not belong to a scout group. When I went to the grub tent to get a tin of cakes that my Mother had baked for us, the tin was there, but the cakes were gone.

I awoke just as it got light to realize that someone had let the tent down and pulled it away by a few yards. We re-erected our tent and walked over to light the fire. It was then that we saw all of our bikes hanging high up in the trees, tied with sisal. We got two of them down safely, but whilst I was gently lowering the third bike [belonging to Higgo], the sisal snapped, and the bike dropped about 20 feet to the ground. There was an awful crunch as the bike landed wheels first. Higgo immediately began to shout at me, calling me names and berating me for damaging his bike.

Both wheels on Higgo's bike were badly buckled, and he was clearly upset. I snapped back at him, saying that I had not purposely or carelessly damaged his bike and that I had been trying to carefully lower it down. It was NOT my fault the bloody sisal had snapped. What did he expect me to do – leave it up there? Higgo couldn't ride his bike because it was so damaged. He borrowed mine and went to the phone box in the nearby village to ask his Dad if he could fetch it in his car. No sooner had Higgo returned to camp still snivelling than his Dad turned up in his car.

I knew Mr. Higginson well. He was a Sunday school teacher at the church I attended every week. He got out of his car and made a beeline for me. This wasn't the benign Mr. Higginson I knew from the Burbage Congregational Church. This wasn't Mr. Higginson who shared a joke with us. This wasn't Mr. Higginson who talked to us about tolerance and forgiveness and love. This was an angry Mr Higginson, who I barely recognized. "Just look at David's bike Dennis. I am not happy about this at all. It's David's pride and joy. How did you come to damage it?" "I DIDN'T damage it. It wasn't my fault Mr. Higginson. It wasn't me who hauled the bike up the tree using sisal. Sisal is not strong enough to guarantee holding bikes. I was trying to help David get it down, but the sisal snapped."

I didn't feel that Mr. Higginson was really listening. "Who is going to pay for this damage?" he demanded."
"Well, not me." I cried, "It wasn't my fault."
"Well, I'll be having a serious talk with Ken Reece about this." And with that, he put the bike in the back of his large car, signalled his son to get in and drove off without another word.

Oh no, no, no, no, no, no, I thought. What the hell will Ken Reece think? Yet another fiasco involving Dennis Perkins. That's what he'll think. It's just not fair. Then there were three. We had another night to go and another day. I spoke to the other two remaining scouts. They both agreed it wasn't my fault, but it didn't move the huge black cloud that was floating just above my head and following me around. We had no way of knowing if our night-time visitors were still on site, and we all felt deflated and disappointed. We decided to call it a day.

I never heard another word from anyone regarding this issue. My guess is that Mr. Higginson calmed down. Questioned his son David again. Realized that it was not my fault and did not mention me to Ken Reece. When I next saw him at Burbage Congs, he was pleasant enough towards me and never mentioned the incident again.

Midnight Hikes

There was one activity I really did enjoy, and that was the occasional night hikes for Patrol Leaders and seconds, which were organized by Ken Reece. I put my name down for every one of them. Parents were asked to drop us off at our Burbage hut [headquarters] at 11:30pm on a Friday night. We had our own rucksacks with spare clothes, wash kit and bedroll. At midnight we would strike off on foot for Fox Covert's campsite on the other side of Kirkby Mallory. When we got to Earl Shilton, Ken Reece always saw to it that there were hot drinks from flasks and a bar of chocolate each [for energy]. When we got to the campsite in the early hours, Ken Reece unlocked the Warden's Hut, where he had stored tents and equipment earlier

that day. This was all arranged via the duty Warden. Ken Reece always planned every detail of our activities meticulously. I particularly enjoyed these night hikes when it snowed. Apart from the excitement this brought to a young boy, it made wildlife easier to spot.
We would usually spend Saturday on some aspect of training. It might be tree or bird recognition. It might be making camp furniture from scout poles and sisal. It might be axeman-ship or cooking. There was usually an exercise involving a problem like moving a heavy object or coping with imaginary disasters such as fire or floods. Saturday night, we were allowed a binge night with hot drinks near a roaring campfire and sweets, cake and biscuits.

Sunday was always a time to polish our shoes and put on our best uniform. It was a part parade and part worship, usually at the camp chapel. Ken Reece would arrange for a lay preacher to pop in to preside over one hymn, [no accompanying music] prayers and a short sermon. After that, we would cook a proper Sunday lunch on an altar fire. Then the washing up and packing up would begin. We had to be ready for our parents, who picked us up at 5:00 pm.

Hinckley District Scouts' campsite at Fox Coverts has provided camping opportunities for young people since 1956. It is located between the villages of Kirkby Mallory and Newbold Verdon in the East Midlands county of Leicestershire but is also close to good road links. Covering nearly 16 acres of woodland, there are campsite areas to suit both group camps and patrol camps, including secluded sites in wooded glades, which are ideal for backwoods, camping and constructing bivouacs.

Patrol Leader and Seconds Training Camps

The Otter Patrol had lost its PL, who had outgrown the scout movement and begun his working life. I was elevated directly to that post. I joined a long weekend training camp, during which I managed to get into trouble with Ken Reece again. The PL and

Second for each patrol [Otters, Beavers, Owls, Swifts, etc.] camped in Black's "Good Companion" two-man tents for this training weekend. For some reason which has disappeared in the mists of time, I did not have a Second with me, so I was in a two-man tent alone. The weather was dodgy, and I expected rain at night, so I gathered kindling and small firewood and put it in my tent to keep it dry. I wasn't going to struggle to light a fire the next day.

We had been kept busy and put through our paces during training on the first day. After the time-honoured supper and sing-song around the campfire, I was glad to turn in and hit the sack at about 10:00 pm. Now, my Mother or my Father, or indeed anyone who had been on holiday with me, could have told Ken Reece that I was NOT a morning person in those days. So when, as part of the training, a scouter, Michael Hunter, woke me at 2:00 am, I was definitely NOT amused. "What?"

"There's a flood. Water is rising behind you. You need to move your tent six feet forward," explained Michael, "and there's no light. We have removed your battery lamps". Not realizing at first that it was a ruse, just for training, I tried to open my eyes as I dragged myself out of my tent. It was a few minutes before I managed to open one eye by just a crack.

"No water here," I bellowed, "Just do it," instructed Michael Hunter.

"NO"

"Okay, I'll fetch Ken Reece then."

"You can fetch the bleedin' Queen for all I care."

I was just drifting off to sleep again when Ken Reece arrived, "Mr Perkins, please move your tent six feet forward."

"NO"

"A scout obeys the orders of his Parents, Patrol Leader, and Scoutmaster without question," reminded Ken sternly, quoting from the Scout Law. "This one doesn't," I mumbled, feeling really irritable. "Well then, this one will be in trouble when I have to explain why I have woken his father and have got him up out of bed at this unearthly hour in the morning to return his son, who has been suspended from the Scout movement and has come last in the PL and Second's Training Camp competition" and with that, Ken left the scene as I, awake by now, had already begun to regret my behaviour. I rolled up my tent brailings and dragged my groundsheet and everything on it forward by six long paces. I then re-pitched the tent over the groundsheet. It took about fifteen minutes

The PL and Second of the Owl Patrol were next to me and were the least experienced. They asked me to give them a hand. We got the groundsheet six feet forward and were just letting the tent down. I was holding the tent up by the main guy rope.

"Are you ready?" I yelled impatiently as the Second fumbled about inside the tent. After a few seconds, he crawled out and cried, "YES." I let go of the main guy rope, and immediately, there was a startling whoosh, and flames flickered around a rapidly enlarging hole in the side of the tent. It was like the opening credit of Bonanza on TV. I dropped the tent flat and stamped on the area which was alight. The flames flickered and smouldered but were quickly extinguished. Even so, there was a black-edged gaping hole in the side of the tent, large enough for me to put my head through and stare at the Second. "You dropped the tent on my candle," he stammered. I was furious. "You lit a bloody candle inside a bloody tent? You bloody idiot," I yelled at him.

Ken Reece must think I am a jinx. He knew I was not directly responsible but was following on from my previous dreadful behaviour. There was little doubt about what was going through Ken's mind. This was yet another unpleasant incident involving Dennis Perkins, who, after points were deducted as a punishment for disobeying Ken Reece, did indeed come last in the competition. I felt totally dejected and ashamed. It was a worry to me. I had such a high opinion of Ken Reece. Obviously, he must have such a low opinion of me.

The Camp Bank

In the evening, we usually had free time, and the tuckshop would open, and we would sign a cheque for a Mars Bar and a bag of Smiths crisps with a little blue screw [bag] of salt. When promoting the advantages of the camp bank, Ken Reece usually included the story of a scout who went to a camp in the late 1950s. Before Ken Reece devised the Camp bank, scouts carried a bundle of notes, their spending money for the week. There was this one lad who had. We'll say, £5.00 spending money which was a lot in those days. Unchecked by an adult, on the first day, he spent Four Pounds and 10 Shillings [£4.50] on a camera. He said, "I love this camera, and I don't care that I will run out of tuck money and that I will not be able to spend any money on anything else. I will save Ten Bob for food on the big day out, and I will manage."
He was ok at first but then the sight of his mates chomping on chocolate bars and slurping Jusoda, Vimto and Tizer drinks sort of got to him, so he sold the camera to another scout for Four Pounds. The next day the camera changed hands for a further reduced amount and so on until by the end of the week, the camera had had about six owners and one smart guy, having carefully budgeted for each day, took it home on the last day having bought it for Nine shillings and sixpence [47.5p] A bargain.

Camp Salisbury

I was lucky enough to squeeze in attendance at four annual camps with the Scouts. The first one was near Salisbury. We did some hiking on the plain. My parents were going on holiday [I cannot remember where] whilst I was going to this camp. As they wanted to leave on Friday night, they arranged for me to stay with a mate of

Dad's who had two sons also going to the camp. I was still painfully shy then and was dropped off at about 5:00 pm and would have an evening meal with this family. I was so shy and mortified that I almost ran away. To make matters worse, I had only moved up to the scouts a few weeks before. I had still not got to know everyone. I also disliked my aloof and very serious Patrol Leader, and the feeling was mutual. I was bullied by the PL, and this snowballed as others joined in, lambasting me at every opportunity, often slagging me off because I lived in a prefab.

On the second day, I was offered a ride on what we then called the aerial runway. They are better known nowadays as zip wires. I was pulled up on the pulley rope by 3 or 4 scouts from the crowd, sitting on a short length of wood until I was about 30 feet up near the top of the tree it was anchored to. Then to my dismay, they wrapped the rope around a smaller tree at the bottom, tied it, and suddenly, everyone disappeared. I was left dangling on my own. Time ticked by, it got cold and dark, and I had a numb bum, and my arms and legs ached, and I was so miserable I wanted to go home.

Eventually, a scout from my patrol wandered by and heard me crying to myself.

"What's going on? Why are you up there, Den? He quickly called a couple of lads from our patrol. They untied and unwound the rope and began to let me down slowly. His name was Alan Linnet. His nickname was Sennit. I have no idea why. He became my friend, and we hung out together for the rest of the camp, and he supported me by encouraging me to stand up to the bullies. He put himself on the line by defending me and berating them for bullying. He was a comical character, and we had some good laughs. I was very grateful to him for turning things around so that after a couple of days, I enjoyed the remaining days at camp and especially our big day out in Bournemouth.

It was one of Ken Reece's strictest rules that we kept our best uniform clean. It was only worn when we went off-site for hikes or church, or visits to places. I inadvertently got my best uniform shirt dirty on my first camp. Ken Reece was not happy at all, and I had to do every piece of washing up for the Otter Patrol for every meal that day.

I also got into trouble for using an axe to chop down a long overhanging branch. I had failed to appreciate that as I had not yet passed my axeman-ship badge, I had no business using an axe. Furthermore, had I gone through the proper training and gained my axeman-ship badge, I would have known that it is only permissible for scouts to cut dead wood. Ken Reece was properly annoyed with me now, and my punishment this time was to saw fifty logs that evening. I was shown a pile of dead tree branches and given a lesson on how to use a bow saw safely. I was given a pattern log so that I could saw the 50 logs to a similar length. It took up most of the evening, during which the others had free time and were enjoying a game of camp cricket. By the time I had finished, my hands were sore, and my back ached. I washed just in time for the drink and light supper which we were allowed. I remember sleeping very well that night.

Another incident that comes to mind at that first camp happened as the Otter Patrol began to line up for inspection. Our sleeping tent, grub tent, the site, the altar fire and all our equipment was clean and tidy. Our personal kit is laid out on the Icelandic groundsheet in the prescribed pattern. Ken Reece was on his way along the footpath leading to our Patrol site. We stood in a straight line. Our Second was a biggish chap who came from a well-to-do family and lived in a big house. He was always making snide remarks about "people who are dragged up in prefabs." Anyway, at this point, he started to make sure that our line was straight by shoving and punching us. The Second always stood at the opposite end of the line to the PL, with the rest of the Patrol in between.

Ken Reece was just entering the Otter Patrol's site when the Second lifted his leg and gave me a good sideways kick on the bottom. However, having been pushed and punched by this bully boy already, the kick sent my temper shooting off the scale, as did happen every once in a while. No sooner had his foot made contact with my backside than I grabbed his ankle and lifted his foot and leg high off the ground so that he was hopping about, trying to remain upright. Just as Ken Reece looked up to address us, I yanked his foot high up into the air, and he sprawled forward, landing flat on his face right in front of Ken Reece. "Ooyah," the Second cried as he scrambled, red-faced, to find his feet and return to his place in the line.

"What's going on here?" enquired Ken, who had not seen the kick or my grab and lift, hidden behind us from his view.

"I just stumbled, Ken," replied the Second, more to save his own face than to prevent me from getting into trouble with Ken Reece.

Ken looked a little puzzled and shook his head slightly before continuing to address us.

When the inspection had been completed, Ken was gone. The bully-boy Second approached me and, putting his face close to mine, gave me a push and growled, "If you do that again, I'll beat you black and blue". I pushed him back hard. "You could TRY." Our PL parted us and gave us tasks to do, well away from each other. I was never troubled by the Second again. I just ignored him from that point forwards. As so often happens with bullies, when it comes to the crunch, he was all mouth.

I had been homesick and unhappy at the beginning of Camp Salisbury. I had been bullied, and I had not made myself very popular with Ken Reece. I had made mistakes because others had not told me or explained the rules. Perhaps I was just too thick to be a scout. I had begun to have mixed feelings about the Scout movement. Yet, when I thought about it afterward, I felt that I had made progress. I wouldn't make the same mistakes again. I had stood up to a bully and gained some respect and a slight softening of attitude towards me. Most importantly, I made a good friend in Alan Linnet.

Camp Dulverton

Dulverton is located in North Devon on the edge of Exmoor National Park, not far from Tiverton. A year had passed since Camp Salisbury. I had attended weekend camps at the Scout Campsite at Kirkby Mallory, only about 10 miles from home. I had learned the rules and been trained on how to do things properly. I had gained badges; camp cooking, axeman-ship, rules of health, basic first aid, knot tying, housekeeping, basic sewing, map reading, bird and tree recognition and others. Non-scouting friends at school tended to scoff, especially at the cooking and sewing, etc., but I was certainly more capable of coping with things and looking after myself, and I was generally more confident.

I didn't get into trouble at Camp Dulverton. I really enjoyed myself. The weather was gloriously sunny for the whole week, and I enjoyed hiking and playing camp cricket, football and wide games. I had had a growth spurt since Camp Salisbury, and although there were still a few older lads who were bigger than me, they didn't bother me. I wasn't the new kid anymore, and I felt more accepted. We had a big day out in Ilfracombe with free time. I spent the day with my old pals, Alan Linnet and Bill Smith. This was better.

Crane and Warbler

One year, instead of camping, Ken Reece organized a different sort of holiday for us. He hired two sixty-foot narrowboats named Crane and Warbler. A long convoy of parents drove us all about 22 miles to the boatyard at Braunston near Daventry. We were to sleep on camp beds. During the day, the camp beds were collapsed and stowed with our own personal equipment in lidded compartments running along each side of the boat. These doubled up as benches.

A purpose-made tarpaulin was thrown over a central beam running the length of the cargo area. This was for shelter. On warm days this could be rolled all the way to the bulkhead, and if I remember rightly, there were about 20 of us on each boat, including Scouters. We chugged gently along the Grand Union canal down to Leighton Buzzard

Throughout the week, we all had several turns at steering these great crafts, under the supervision of a scouter, of course. Inevitably, in the beginning, there were one or two groundings and bumps. One scout, who shall remain nameless, actually knocked down a small tree about eight feet inland, but we soon had the hang of it. Incredibly, all the cooking was done in the tiny galley near the stern. There were six propane burners above the shallow oven, a narrow shelf and a small seat. Two people could just about squeeze in there. Again, we all took several turns cooking meals and sat next to a scouter. The food would then be plated onto enamel plates and would be passed "forward" using a human chain. Our tea and coffee, as at ordinary camps, would be in our own enamel mug.

We soon became proficient at passing through canal locks. The leading narrowboat would cut the engine just before the lock. The trailing narrowboat would pull alongside, and ropes would be thrown across. The two boats would be lashed together to save time. Only one boat would have throttle and steering at this point and would be in control of both boats going into the lock. Once we got through, the leading boat would restart its engine and take the lead again. My mate, Bill Smith, was travelling on Warbler, which was the lead boat, and I was on board Crane, the trailing boat. When the boats went through locks, we often took the opportunity to have a chat. We would meet both of us amidships would have one foot on each boat facing each other. One day we were engrossed in a conversation, and as the two boats drifted apart and Warbler moved ahead to lead, we both toppled over and landed in the canal. It was a fairly common occurrence, and our mates pulled us out. We had to dry ourselves. Then wrung out our wet clothes and sat in dry underpants in the corner of the hold where nobody would see us until our clothes were dried on the galley oven. It took less than an hour.

We were cruising along one day when we heard a loud voice shouting for help. We recognized the loud voice as belonging to Dave (Higgo) Higginson, but despite everyone running around and listening for his cries and looking for him, we couldn't find him. Then a sharp-eyed scout noticed two hands right at the point of the bow. Poor old Higgo. Unnoticed by anyone, he had lost his balance and fallen but managed to hang on. As the boat was moving forward, he was facing backward, hanging on to the bow for dear life. His legs were trailing in the water on each side of the bow, and he was afraid that if he let go, he would be "run over" by the boat.

We were drifting peacefully along one day, and I was taking my turn to do the drying up after the main meal of the day. I had stacked all the dry pots, pans, plates, cups and cutlery when suddenly, **WHOOSH**. My breath was taken away as cold canal water came cascading all over me and the clean, dry pans. We had been the subject of a surprise water raid from the bridge we had just gone underneath, carried out by those pesky varmints on Warbler who had jumped on the towpath, dipped buckets, and any other vessel they could lay their hands on into the canal ran to the bridge and as we passed under let us have the lot, the sods.

Ever since getting told off by Ken Reece on my first camp for getting my best uniform shirt dirty, I always made damn sure that I kept my uniform hung up and clean. On the Sunday morning of our Narrowboat adventure, we were all scrubbed up in our best uniforms with polished black shoes and almost ready to go to church in a nearby village near our mooring. Ken Reece looked at his usual smart self and gave us the "five minutes before we march" signal. All the scouts had begun to line up in marching order. A scouter and a senior scout had a special dispensation to miss church in order to cook dinner for us all. Ken was giving them last-minute instructions and putting on his scout beret. There was a mirror hung on the side of the boat, and he looked in it to check his beret and straighten his neckerchief. He turned to speak to someone, then took a step backward – right into the canal and DISAPPEARED UNDER WATER.

For a split second, about a dozen nearby scouts all froze in their tracks, horror-stricken, mouths agape and eyes bulging wide open. This could NOT be happening. NOT to Ken Reece. I was a trained lifesaver then, but I wasn't the only one who kicked off their shoes, ready to enter the canal if necessary. Anyone who has entered a canal will know that there can be up to a foot of soft mud at the bottom. Unknown to me at that time, of all the things, Ken could not swim. He had tried to push up with his feet but sank further into the mud. Three of us were just going in when up he popped, having freed himself. He spluttered and coughed up water and held up his arms. They were grabbed by many helping hands, and he was hauled out of the water even faster than he went in. He soon recovered, but he had had a fright. He was upset that he could not now lead the march to church with a wet and slimy green uniform.

Despite our skirmishes [mainly due to my own bad behaviour], I had always liked Ken, and despite everything, I did respect him. In many ways, I had begun to appreciate and admire him for how he did things. I did not want to see him upset in this way. Thankfully, by the time we got back from church, he had found a nearby boater's shower block, showered and changed into his casual [but warm and dry] camp clothes. One of the Scouters had made him a huge mug of tea, and he had smoked two or three Park Drive cigarettes. Thank goodness Ken Reece was okay.

As he began making tea for everyone else, I couldn't resist it. "Don't spill your tea," I said to nobody in particular but within his earshot. "There are rules about getting your best uniform dirty" He took it in good spirit, and as he fixed me with a pretend glare, he quipped, "Ha ha. Mr. Perkins – you won't want any lunch then, will you? Just in case you spill it on your uniform" We all laughed. Everything was alright. Ken Reece was ok and back on form. We all enjoyed a lovely Sunday roast lunch which we ate, having changed back into our camping clothes. We marvelled that it had all been produced in two very small narrow boat galleys on board Crane and Warbler. The new kind of scouting holiday had been a success. Everyone had a cracking time

Camp Grasmere

This was my first camp as a Patrol Leader. It was a long journey made in a box lorry. I managed to get a seat at the rear of the vehicle. The roller shutter was left up, and a row of bare knees [in shorts] were jammed against the tailgate. Bill Smith sat next to me, and at one point, he looked down at the row of knees and scratched my knee instead of his own. I had never been to the Lake District before, and I just fell in love with the whole area. I had always loved the countryside around the home, but this area had hills and lakes and rivers and so much natural beauty. I was enchanted. The campsite was just outside Grasmere and was situated halfway up a green hill.

There were two separate flat levels, one above the other, for pitching tents. The upper one swept around in a sort of semi-circle large enough for four areas to be roped off with sisal. One for each patrol and each large enough to comfortably accommodate an eight-man Icelandic ridge tent, a four-foot x six-foot grub tent, an alter fire and sumps, wet and dry, leaving enough room for everyone to move around. Four separate footpaths, one from each Patrol site, lead steeply down some thirty feet to the lower level.

A large grub tent was pitched here behind the general-use Scouter's tent, used for meetings etc. To the East of this area was a square flat area large enough for the whole troop to gather. There was a flag pole in front of which we all gathered when summoned. To the West of this was a slightly smaller flat area upon which four two-man tents were pitched for sleeping four Scouters and three senior

Scouts, one of which was my mate Bill Smith sleeping alone in a two-man tent to the right of the path leading to my Patrol campsite. Bill had become my best mate over the previous couple of years. This school summer holiday, we cycled for miles together, camped, fished local canals, swam at the local baths and visited the local cinemas, and even went to the library. Bill had even been on holiday with my family. Bill was almost a year older than me and had moved up to the Senior Scouts, and I was looking forward to joining him at the end of the year. The scoutmaster for the senior scouts was Ken Wainwright, who we all called Skip. He was a really nice bloke.

We did some fell walking under supervision. I loved it. It was so breathtakingly beautiful over the fells. We visited Grasmere, Ambleside and Windermere. We enjoyed a boat trip. We visited 'Dove Cottage' where the poet William Wordsworth had lived. I loved it all.

I wandered, lonely as a cloud
That floats on high o'er vales and hills,
When all at once, I saw a crowd,
A host of golden daffodils;
Beside the Lake, beneath the trees,
Fluttering and dancing in the breeze

William Wordsworth 1770 - 1850

I was 15 years of age now and already a smoker. One evening a mate of mine overheard the Scouters talking about their suspicions that I was smoking and planning a surprise raid on the Otter Patrol's personal equipment in the hope of finding and confiscating my cigarettes. When my mate told me of this, I remember thinking that I could not afford to let them do that. I removed a small toffee tin from my rucksack, put my pack with seven cigarettes inside it and hid it, buried in a shallow hole in the long grass underneath a nearby bush.

Sure enough, the raid came the next day. The scouter and policeman strode quickly, quietly and unexpectedly into the Otter Patrol camp. He immediately proceeded with a comprehensive search of my personal belongings [nobody else's]. When he couldn't find anything, he didn't seem at all pleased and issued me with a warning that if I was found with cigarettes, they would be confiscated. As I understood it at the time, there was a law against selling cigarettes to anyone below the age of 16 years. As far as I knew, there was no law against underage persons actually smoking them. I may have been wrong, of course, but thinking along those lines at the time, I felt that this had been a personal grudge thing because he did not like me and that he was in the wrong and being unfair by trying to steal my cigarettes. Thus, the relationship between this scouter / policeman and me, never very good, suddenly took a turn for the worse.

However, a few evenings later, I could not help but appreciate his speed of thought and action [police training, no doubt] as I watched him deal with an emergency. The Beaver Patrol were making their way down the footpath to the gathering place near the flagpole. Partway down the hill, one scout suddenly turned and ran back up the hill as if he had forgotten something and was returning to retrieve it. A few minutes later, he came back into view. In order to catch up with his Patrol, he decided to ignore the footpath and started to run down the hill through the thick bracken.

Unfortunately, he ran straight through a nest of hornets, causing them to swarm after him. He was stung all over his body. I had one single hornet sting once, and I can tell you they are really painful. This poor boy had scores of them. He screamed as he continued to run to the bottom, where Gordon Gibbons happened to be. As the screaming scout approached him, Gordon yanked his top off over his head. He then took the scout by the hand and ran with him quickly the few yards to the scouter's tent. Reaching inside, he found what he wanted - a fly spray. Close your eyes tightly, he shouted and sprayed up and down, close to but not directly onto, the boy's body and kept spraying until the spray ran out. "Fetch dixie cans of water" yelled Gordon taking the boy into the Scouter's tent for privacy.

His shorts and pants were removed, and he was doused in water and then covered with clean towels. He began to struggle for breath and was going into shock. His body was covered in stings. After getting him to breathe deeply, Gordon and another scouter [both trained in first aid] carried the scout to Gordon's car, and they sped along the track leading to the road. In those days, before mobile phones, it was quicker to take him to "Casualty," as it was called then, before they renamed it "A and E." It was the end of the lad's holiday. He was properly poorly. His parents travelled up to the Lake District, and when the hospital discharged him a couple of days later, they took him home to recuperate. It was a shock for all of us.

A couple of nights later, after lights out at 10:00 pm, I crawled out of our patrol tent and, keeping an eye out for Scouters and keeping low, I crept down the path using the ferns as cover. I was headed for Bill Smith's tent. He was in a two-man tent on his own, so occasionally, I would nip down late at night, and we would have a chat [in whispers], have a smoke together, and then I would sneak back to my tent. This particular night though, the Scouters and the Senior Scouts were still in the Scouter's Tent, all chatting and enjoying a warm drink. I was just wondering whether to return to my tent when senior scouts and Scouters came out of the Scouter's tent [used for meetings etc., and not for sleeping] and began to make their way to their own tents. I was in the line of vision, so I quickly undid the door to Bill's tent and slid in. I pulled a blanket over me just in case someone peeped in.

Eventually, all the Goodnight calls gradually ceased, and Bill pushed his head into the tent. It was pitch black, and as he searched for his torch amongst the blankets, I spoke in a hoarse whisper. "What time do you call this?" There was a sharp intake of breath, and clutching his heart Bill fell to the ground, moaning softly. I ignored him and found his torch. I switched it on and noticed that his face was a whiter shade of pale.

“Fancy a smoke, Bill?”

“No, you barmy bastard, you frit the living daylights out of me. I nearly shit myself. Bugger off”

He then began to punch and kick at me, so I escaped and scarpered back to my tent. Bill had obviously temporarily forgotten the tenth Scout Law.

10. A scout is clean in thought, WORD, and deed.

The next day we were friends again. I apologised and explained that I hadn’t realized how much I had scared him. We laughed about his shock, and we laughed about him lashing out at me and especially about me running away. I still laugh when I think of it now, fifty-odd years later. Sadly, I lost touch with Bill over the years. He moved out of the area where we lived, and I had not seen him for about fifty years. I have no idea where Bill is or even if he is still alive. I often think of him. In the words of the famous old Carlsberg TV advert,
“Bill Smith - probably the best mate in the world.”

Scout Pantomimes

Skip Wainwright was very good at scriptwriting our pantomimes. His scripts were clear for everyone to follow, with some really funny bits in. There were always songs to learn too. We would perform in local village halls, huts, and church halls and especially, we would put on several performances, including matinees, at our local Conservative Club Hut. Which was bigger and better than the description “hut” implies. It even had a proper stage with rooms on either side backstage. We had parental helpers to make props and costumes, and one of the Cub’s Dad was even a dab hand with

theatrical make-up. We raised money for camping equipment and even gave some to charity.
I never played a leading part. In my first one, I was just a "crowd extra" in a couple of scenes. My best effort was as a blonde Dutch dancing girl. I had to learn a song or two and the dance, which was properly choreographed. My apparent sex change caused some ribald banter from mates, particularly non-scouting mates. I handled it well, though, and basically ignored them all. The acting was never really my thing, but there was a bonus this year.

One of the Senior Scouts had a sister who played the lead female role in all our pantomimes. She was a little older than me, and her name was Catherine. She was the loveliest girl and had the most beautiful smile. Several times during rehearsals, pantomime producer Skip Wainwright had to tell me to close my mouth, stop staring at Catherine, stop being gormless and pay attention to what he was saying. Mind you. I wasn't the only one. She was such a nice person and captivated everyone. I think most of us fell under her charming spell. I certainly fell a little bit in love with her.

The final performance was on a Saturday night. As I allowed myself a pre-show peep through the curtain at the audience, I was horrified to spot my school teacher, Mr. Briggs, sitting there with his family, waiting for the show to begin. He was my favourite teacher, but that made it even worse. My nerve almost went. I had to gather up my confidence and just get on with it. Somehow, I managed to get through it.

Back at school on Monday, after assembly and prayers, etc., we began lessons properly. Mr. Briggs told us to get our 'News Books' out (a sort of occasional Diary) and write a few pages about what we had done at the weekend. After a while, Mr. Briggs selected a few of us to read out our entries to the class. After half a dozen kids had stumbled and stammered, reading out loud as they struggled to read their own writing.

Someone asked Mr. Briggs what he had done at the weekend. This was a popular timewaster Mr. Briggs was talking and answering questions about his weekend. We did not actually have to do any work. "What did you do at the weekend, Sir?" asked one of the girls. An alarm went off in my head. Oh No! Would he mention our pantomime? Oh my God, will he mention me? Surely not. Shall I quickly go to the bogs and avoid major embarrassment? But before I could, Mr. Briggs answered the girl.

"I went to see a wonderful pantomime which was performed by the local Boy Scouts," began Mr. Briggs cheerfully. "It was really good ....and DENNIS, I must say" [looking directly at me] "YOU MADE A LOVELY DANCING GIRL" The class erupted into loud hoots of laughter as I shrank lower into my seat and simultaneously made a passable impression of a tomato.

SENIOR SCOUTS

I moved up to Senior Scouts when I was about 15 years old. Once again, there were tests to pass. One was an eight-mile hike, with another senior scout, following written instructions and map references, gathering evidence on-route, and camping overnight, cooking our own meals. It was good to get with my old mate Bill Smith again. Since he was a few months older than me, he had been elevated to a senior scout before me. I had missed him. On the downside, there were only about six of us. There had been a big fall-off in attendance as lads began work and/or studying for exams etc., or became more interested in girls. Within a couple of months, there was only me and Bill left. Ken Wainwright [Skip] was running what was left of things, assisted by a scouter called Mick Vardon, another nice bloke. We all got along famously and decided to carry on for a while to see if things improved. Formalities were dropped. For instance, we came to the meetings in casual clothes. The activities were tailored to suit the four of us too.

One night, Bill and I were treated, from Scout funds to a bottle of coke and a bag of crisps, and we spent all night playing card games. Another time Bill and I took our Scalextric car racing track and cars to the scout hut, put them together to make one huge track and had a great night. Even skip enjoyed it. He had never played at Scalextric before. We did that several times over the winter nights. Sometimes Ken Reece would send word and ask if we could please clean or repair some camping equipment or dry out some tents etc. We were happy to help. One night I got my Dad to take my drums up to the hut, and Bill bought his guitar for a music night. One night we went to the cinema to see a James bond film. I'm fairly sure it was Thunder Ball. If the Burbage Old Boys (local football team) had a mid-week fixture, we occasionally would watch the match and pick up a bag of chips afterward. In the summer, we would often go for a walk.

Skip was ill for a while, and whilst it was nothing serious, it took him a few weeks to get over it. I'm fairly sure it was around the same time that Mick's relationship with his girlfriend got a bit more serious as they became engaged to be married.

The 1st Burbage Senior Scout Troop just ground to a halt. It was a shame but inevitable in a way. I have a few bad memories from all my days in the Boy Scout Movement but tons of happy ones.

So much so that years later, when my son became the right age, I encouraged him to join the Cubs. Like me, he was shy, and he wasn't sure. His birthday was in January, but the Scoutmaster from the 11th Hinckley Methodist Scout Group came to have a chat and invited Kevin to the Cubs' Christmas Party. This would enable Kevin to get to know one or two and help ease him into the Cubs. I picked him up after the party, and on the way home, I asked how he had liked it.

"I definitely want to join Cubs, Dad," was his enthusiastic reply. "I am pleased, Kevin. You weren't sure before. Something must have impressed you. What changed your mind?"

"It was great Dad. There was this kid, and he ate a mince pie and a pickled onion AT THE SAME TIME."

DYB DYB DYB DYB. [Do Your Best]

The legendary Scoutmaster, Ken Reece, at a fundraising fete on Burbage Old Boys field.

A scout panto at the Grove Road Hut

Ist Burbage. Otter Patrol c1965. Taken at Fox Coverts Campsite

Back Row Left to Right David Higginson, Myself [Patrol Leader] Richard Maycock

Front Row Left to Right Michael Wormleighton, Geoff Maycock, Steve Tyler

ALL GOOD OLD BURBAGE BOYS

CHAPTER TEN: HASTINGS HIGH SCHOOL

Hastings High was huge. Much bigger and more modern than I was used to. You could easily get lost until, in time, you found your way around. The Head in September 1962, when I first attended the school, had been a war hero, an officer. He dressed impeccably and spoke perfect English in short, rapid-fire staccato sentences. I once overheard a teacher saying that he was a cold fish and never showed emotion. I would go a step further. He was ice cold towards us all. His Deputy, on the other hand, was much more human. His name was Mr. Hughes and he was nicknamed "Bomber" by the students. He was quite hard but fair. He also had a sense of humour, unlike the Head. The girls had their own Deputy Head, Mrs. Jenkins. My Form teacher, to whom I reported each morning for registration, was Mr. Duckham. Students then worked to a timetable, moving from room to room to be taught different subjects by different teachers. It was a disciplined environment, and the rules were strict.

Bad Behaviour

I have to be honest. I was not well-behaved during my time at Hastings High School. I often played truant. My usual trick was to register my presence after morning assembly at 9:00 am and then, choosing the lessons run by teachers who had less control than others, would sneak off school premises. The best route was to make sure there were no teachers in the tennis courts, which doubled as a playground at break times. Also, none were standing on the steps leading down from the rear doors to the main building. Usually, a mate or two would move quickly behind the bike sheds out of sight of the school, then run down the grass embankment, which ran all the way along behind three full-size tennis courts and went downwards some 15 feet or more.

Although we had a six-foot chain link face to climb over, the depth of the grass bank at this point meant that we could not be seen from the school buildings. We dropped from the top of the fence onto the lash hill footpath and ran down a few yards, dodged left, and through a gap in the hedge. Then down another eight-foot bank, we'd hide behind a row of garages. Once we got our breath back, we would then head for wherever we had decided to spend the rest of the morning. We got rumbled a couple of times and ended up in the Head's office. On one occasion, I told him I had forgotten to tell my form teacher that I had a dental appointment. Whilst he was ranting at us, he pulled out a dental appointment card from my blazer top pocket. I had previously nicked this card from the dentist and had filled in fictitious appointment details for that morning.

Teachers

Teachers were still allowed to clout kids in those days, and I earned quite a lot of corporal punishment. One lunchtime, a teacher knocked me for six with a backhander. I had been home during the lunch hour for a bite to eat, and as it was a hot day, once I was home, I had removed my school tie. I put it in my blazer pocket so that I would not forget it when I returned to school. School ties had to be worn at all times. As I walked into the main entrance, there was a coach parked up. Some lucky kids were going on a field trip. This teacher came from behind the coach, and **BANG**, I was decked. I had simply forgotten to put my tie back on.

The PE teacher Mr. Onions was the smallest teacher but the heaviest handed. He often clouted boys for no reason at all. He would turn off the heat for the showers before we had finished rinsing down, so not only did we get momentarily deluged with ice-cold water, we hadn't been able to rinse all the soap off. If you forgot your P.E. kit, he laid into you and made you wear a pair of disgusting dirty shorts from lost property. He was mean and sadistic.

Mr. Roe, our science teacher, was a fair man, but if you crossed him, he would use a meter rule for a cane. Bent over a laboratory stool. The first stroke wasn't too bad. However, he was a marksman, and the second stroke would thud against your buttocks in exactly the same place and sting you like hell. The third stroke, again in exactly the same place, would always make you shout out in pain and make your eyes water. He seldom gave more than three strokes. That was enough. Mr. Roe rode a motor scooter and, in my last term at Hastings High School, would come into my father's shop to purchase a ten-pack of cigarettes. He often gave me a lift to school on the pillion of his scooter, and on my last day, I paid for ten cigarettes out of my pocket money, and my Mum gave them to him when he came into the shop. Back at school, he sent for me and thanked me very much. Despite the meter rule discipline, I liked and respected him. He never punished me for no reason. With Mr. Roe, I'm afraid that I always had it coming.

Mr. Compton, the Welsh woodwork teacher, would grab a bit of hair at the side of your head and twist it and twist it until you yelped. Another favourite punishment of his was to make you hold the "long clamp" used for clamping wood together whilst glue set. He would make you hold them away from your body with your arms held straight outwards at shoulder height. If you lowered your arms as they began to ache, he would clout your arse with a length of wooden dowelling. "Get your arms up," he would yell. One day, whilst administering this punishment, he went too far for a student called John Gardener. John threw the clamp at Mr. Compton [luckily, it missed] and vented his outrage by shouting that he did not come to school to be treated like this and would not be attending any more lessons. "My Dad can teach me all the woodwork I need to know," he yelled. Mr. Compton backed off and took John into his little office.

They must have resolved their issues because John continued with Mr. Compton's woodwork lessons.

I got into trouble several times for smoking. Most teachers would send you to Bomber Hughes for punishment. He would tell me how bad smoking was for me. Have you any more cigarettes on you? He would say. Sometimes I had a chance to give fags and/or matches to a mate to keep for me as I walked to Bomber's office. Occasionally I had to give them to less-than-trustworthy individuals, and that would sometimes result in a fight to get them back. Bomber would then ask where we got the fags from. Where did we get the money from to buy them and so on? Some teachers were unorthodox. One such was Mr. Shenton, himself a smoker, whose car broke down one day and caused him to walk to school, passing right by our smoking place a quarter of a mile away from school just as I was about to light a fag which dangled from the corner of my mouth. He stood where he was, perhaps thirty feet away from me, and held out his hand. I walked over to him and placed the fag in his upturned hand.

"Got any more cigarettes, Perkins?" he inquired.

"No, Sir."

"Pity.......Got a light?"

Towards the end of my first year at Hastings High School, we sat exams, and a few weeks later, I was told that after the holiday, I would start the new term in Class 2C. I was pleased, and looking back, I wonder what I could have achieved if I had put some proper effort into my schoolwork. One day, at about 4:00 pm, I was on my way home and lit up a fag when an elderly maths teacher (who did not teach me) called Mrs. Downes, who also smoked, suddenly came around the corner going back to school. I have no idea why. Maybe she had forgotten something. Not having time to clip out the lit cigarette before she saw me, I cupped it in my hand and put my hand in my blazer side pocket. As she approached me, she shook her head disapprovingly.

"That's the best way to set fire to yourself, you blithering idiot," she informed me loudly but carried on walking past me without confiscating my cigarettes. Nor did she report me. Maybe she was in a hurry. She wasn't one of my teachers, but I liked her more following this incident.

Some months later, I came across her walking the same way as me to catch a bus. The bus stop was quite a distance away, and she was carrying two heavy briefcases and a shoulder bag. She graciously accepted my offer of help, and I carried both briefcases to the bus stop for her. As we made our way, we engaged in a conversation about Leicester City Football Club, and I was surprised by her in-depth knowledge. Once at the bus stop, I was glad to put down the heavy briefcases and take a breather. She looked me in the eye. "Thank you, young man. You have helped me considerably," and thereafter, whenever I saw her in the school corridors, she would give a slight nod towards me with a mere trace of a smile. I felt I had repaid a kindness to a very likable lady.

My own maths teacher, although very stern and fiery, had a sense of humour too. He was a hard man, and his name was Mr. Garner. I was always in trouble for not doing homework which I generally despised. It was my considered opinion that we did enough work in the day at school without teachers stealing my free time to do more work yet. All I wanted to do when I arrived home after spending all day cooped up at school was to change out of my uniform and get outside in the fresh air. Also, maths has always been my weak subject because although I could usually get most of the answers, I was painfully slow at working them out.

"Stand up all those who have not done their homework," he bellowed one afternoon. About a dozen students stood up. Mr. Garner's eyes narrowed as he glowered at us. He was obviously annoyed that so many of us had stood up. Once they had given a reason and been excused or punished, they would be told to sit down. I sat at a square table with three mates, two facing two. After a while, during which you could have heard a pin drop, he addressed our table last of all.

"Hubbard," shouted Mr. Garner, "Why?"

"Please, Sir, I left my book in Perkins's satchel Sir."

"One hundred lines Hubbard and the missing homework by Friday. I must take responsibility for my own books. Sit down."

Dickens, "Why?"

"Please, Sir, I left my book in Perkins's satchel Sir."

Mr. Garner looked very angry as he dished outlines to Dickens too. "Belcher," boomed Mr. Garner over the sniggers of laughter from the class."

"Why?"

"Please, Sir, I left my book in Perkins's satchel Sir.

Rolling his eyes towards the ceiling, Mr. Garner metered out the same punishment to Belcher.

By this time, I was a bit worried, not to mention flabbergasted. In fact, my flabber had never been so gasted. Not one of the rotten sods had left their maths book in my satchel at all. This was serious. With mates like this, who needed enemies? What the hell was I going to say to retrieve this situation?

There was quite a long pause as if Mr. Garner was trying to regain control of his temper. Eventually, he eyed me coldly.

"Come on then, Perkins. Let's have it?"

By now, I was the only culprit still left standing. I gulped and pushed my satchel further under the desk with my toe.

"Please, Sir..............well...........er........... I lost the satchel."

The class erupted into hoots of laughter, but Mr. Garner's face set hard. "QUIET," he bellowed.

He glared around. The laughing abruptly ceased. His face went red and then turned to an alarming shade of purple. He seemed to be wrestling with some inner battle. I cringed inside, expecting him to explode with violence at any second. I was tensed, ready to duck or run, or both. After what seemed like an hour but was probably only a minute or two, his normal colour began to return as he regained control of his anger.

"It's a good job. I have a sense of humour, boy. Take 500 lines by Friday. I must not allow other people to put books in my satchel."

"Oh, Sir! 500, Sir? Please, surely not that many? That's very harsh, Sir. I'll be up all night, Sir."

Mr. Garner was unmoved. "Stop whinging, Perkins. Five hundred by Friday - or else." he said sharply, "and the missing homework too, or you are really for it, boy," I mean it. I had no doubt that he meant it.

Another day, I was in metalwork class. I got on well with Mr. Wright, the metalwork teacher. He was another one who passed our shop occasionally on his way to school and would pick me up if he saw me waiting at the bus stop near our shop. Having just finished making a shield-shaped brass lapel badge with my initials on of which I was rather proud, I was waiting in a small line of students to speak to Mr. Wright in order to ask him what my next project was going to be. He would then have given me the metal for it and a drawing and talked me through how to begin to make it. However, I didn't get a chance to speak to him before the Headmaster exploded into the workshop and made a beeline straight for me.

"What are you doing, Perkins?" and before I could even answer him, he began to clout me hard around the head and shoulders whilst shouting at me, "You are doing nothing. You are always doing nothing. You are a lazy, shiftless waste of space, you idle, good for nothing, ne'er do well, useless, tiresome, [the insults kept coming, each one punctuated by clout], spineless, sneaky, workshy, little toad". He stared at me, slightly pop-eyed.

Suddenly, he turned on his heel and marched back out of the workshop, slamming the door behind him. I was dazed and felt as if I'd been three rounds in the ring with Henry Cooper. I sank to the floor and sat with my back leaning against the wall, head in hand. There was a shocked silence at first. No one could quite believe it had happened. One or two close mates murmured, "Bloody hell" – "The bastard." Even Mr. Wright seemed taken aback and a little embarrassed by this unprovoked attack and enquired if I was alright. "Yes, thank you, Sir…….. I think he likes me, really." Everyone laughed, but despite my bravado, I was hurting alright.

I was hauled up in front of Deputy Head Bomber Hughes on another occasion. A tell-tale Prefect had reported me for cycling with more than one person on the bike.

"Now then," boomed Bomber looking at the Prefect. "How many boys were on the bike?"

"Five, Sir," replied the Prefect.

"FIVE?" bellowed Bomber in disbelief, almost deafening me and the Prefect. "…. and was the bike moving quickly?"
"Oh yes, Sir, like a motorbike, Sir. Down Far Lash Hill, Sir, just as a school bus turned out of St Catherine's Way, Sir, there was very nearly a collision."

"Good Heavens," exclaimed Bomber loudly, an incredulous expression on his face. "What do you have to say for yourself, Perkins?"

"Please, Sir, he's exaggerating. It's impossible to get five on a bike. I was just giving my mate a croggy (local slang for a ride on the crossbar). We were going very slowly, and we were nowhere near the bus, Sir." [Another 500 lines. I must not allow my friends to ride on my bike when I am already riding it.] His sardonic humour within the wording of the lines was lost on me in this instance. Bloody Hell, I thought, I'll be writing lines forever. I've only just finished Mr. Garner's 500 lines. When am I supposed to bloody eat and sleep? I remember wishing that I could give lines to the teachers. I must be more lenient when giving out lines because twenty is plenty. However, I can reveal now that the Prefect's version of events was much nearer the truth than mine. It's not easy to get five boys on a moving bike, but we managed it. The trouble was that as we hurtled, wobbling down the hill, I pulled the brake levers as hard as I could, but there was so much weight on the bike the brakes did not work properly. We continued way past where we had planned to draw to a halt. We whizzed over a crossroads just as a school bus was coming the other way. It was a narrow squeak. Still, as I was expecting the cane, I suppose I got away pretty lightly. Once I had calmed down a bit, I remember thinking that Bomber Hughes wasn't so bad. Strangely, he had my respect.

A while later, I let off a twopenny cannon banger [very loud firework], which made the girls scream just as they were coming out of their PE changing room. I wasn't so lucky this time. I was spotted and got six of the best. Three on each hand from Bomber. OUCH! But hell. I soon recovered, so, no complaints. I deserved it, and he had a job to do, so that's fair enough.

I worked hard for Miss Moray and Mr. Roson, my English teachers because I liked the subject and respected them both. Consequently, I came first in English exams every year. The exception was the 3rd year when I came second to a nice girl by the name of Roslyn York. However, I found a genuine error in the teachers marking, received a further three marks, and narrowly leapfrogged into first place again. I'm sorry, Roslyn. The poor girl was rightly delighted to have topped the class in English for all of ten minutes before I stuck my oar in. I hope she didn't hate me too much. I also once got a piece of prose in the school magazine, Hasta 63.

The School Play

I was fortunate enough to avoid being picked for the school play. I could not act for a toffee, and that is still the case now. If I really dislike someone, I cannot hide it because I am incapable of acting or pretending, so I just 'pass them by, as the old song goes. I was always happy enough to go and watch annual school plays. I appreciated the hard work that had gone into every aspect, and I did enjoy them.

The School Dance

I was less fortunate with the annual school dance. PE lessons turned into nightmare ballroom dancing lessons for a month leading up to the school dance. There was no escape, and we were mortified to have to miss football and instead waste our time practicing waltzes and foxtrots and other dances, the names of which I cannot even remember, with girls, for goodness sake. I'm sure the girls were equally mortified to be dancing with us too. Our lessons included manners and etiquette and especially how to ask a lady for a dance and how not to. Attendance was compulsory. We were threatened with unimaginable consequences should we not turn up for practices or the actual dance, and most of all, if we were seen to be hanging around and not asking females to dance in the proper manner. The females in question could be students, teachers, parents, school governors, or invited local dignitaries. I squirmed with embarrassment and shyness for the whole evening as I did just enough to avoid punishment. I was so relieved when it ended. It reminded me of an appropriate poem I read somewhere in a comic. I think it was the Dandy.

My dancing teacher at the school,
Said I am a silly fool,
I should be dainty, but instead,
My feet clump down like lumps of lead.

I came third in the high jump in year one and second in year two. Whilst I was battling for second or third place in year three, I failed to clear the bar, and as I landed on it, the force toppled the upright stand, which then fell on top of me, hitting my head. The stand was heavy and almost knocked me out. I was dazed for a time. A teacher had to take me to hospital for a couple of stitches in my forehead hairline. I also did fairly well in the triple jump, but I can't remember the full details of my positions. I was never any good at sprinting, but when younger, I was strong and had stamina. I was always in the top 15 each time we had a school three-mile cross-country run. I was always up there with the skinny, lanky kids.

The Old Oak

If two boys had a disagreement, rather than risk punishment at school for fighting, we would meet at the "Old Oak," a tree in the middle of a nearby field just out of sight of the school. Interested students who would hear about fights on the grapevine would form a circle around the two fighters. There were no rules, and both contestants would charge in with very little finesse and make a serious attempt to knock lumps out of each other whilst the crowd began shouting encouragement to their preferred fighter. If one fighter got an injury, a nosebleed, say, or a loose tooth or was getting a beating and things looked to be getting out of hand, other students from the circle would stop the fight and announce the winner. The fighters would shake hands, and thus fair play was kept, serious injury avoided and honour maintained. There was always someone to comfort the loser and say what a great fight he had put up even though he had lost.

I was a contender twice. The first time I had somehow managed to upset a guy. He was not in any of my classes, and I did not know him very well. His nickname was Tocker. Tocker Ward. I don't know what his proper forename was. It may have been Tony. I cannot for the life of me remember how I upset him, but he was as mad as hell.

"I'll see you at the Old Oak at Four ['o' Clock], Kid," he snarled through gritted teeth with the emphasis on KID. This was the accepted, time-honoured, traditional school challenge. Word for word repeated many times for many years, I reckon. Even when, the following year, the old oak was felled due to disease; the students of Hastings High School still called that area 'The Old Oak' and held fights there. So anyway, I met Tocker at the Old Oak at four.

Preparations were made, and I waded in with arms flailing like propellers. Poor old Tocker was expecting a boxing match, but that's not what you got at the Old Oak. It was always like a good old western bar brawl. After catching a couple of hefty right hooks from me, Tocker submitted. As often happens, we became friends for the rest of our time at school. When I left Hastings, I lost track of him and know not what became of him, though I often wonder.

My second fight, about a year later, was with a broad, solidly built lad called Andy Millington. I had crept up and knelt behind him as he was watching football. My mate then, from the front, pushed him back over me. Surprisingly, he took strong exception to this, and I, rather than my mate who pushed him, was the target of his anger...

"I'll see you down the Old Oak at four, kid," growled Andy. He looked like a hard case to me, but I agreed because had I not done so, I would have lost credibility, and worse, I would have been called a chicken by all and sundry. That's how it was then. It was a matter of honour like it was with an old-fashioned dual. There was already a huge crowd there when I arrived. A fight involving two biggish, well-built lads always drew more spectators. The circle of people parted to let me through, then closed again behind me.

My heart was thumping away like a drum. I removed my coat and tie, rolled up my sleeves and waded in again with arms flailing, throwing punches left and right. Over went, Andy just like Tocker had done. However, Andy was made of stern stuff because although I had landed several hard punches, he was quickly up again and facing me. He attacked me with his own barrage of blows. He caught me cleanly on the chin with a mighty straight jab which I didn't even see coming. I was poleaxed and went down like a sack of spuds [as we say in Hinckley]. I was a bit dizzy and shocked. To Andy's credit, he stood back, but I didn't immediately realize why. I was struggling to get up and back at him when the fight was stopped by two or three of the older students. I stared down, and to my surprise, my shirt was very bloody. I had not even realized that Andy's jab had been a direct hit to my chin, and my lip had been badly split by my own lower front teeth. Someone knew an off-shift ambulance man living close by, and with an arm on my shoulder, guided me to this man's house and asked for his help. He stopped it from bleeding. I still have a small hard lump in my lip now. Thanks, Andy. If you hadn't split my lip, I reckon I'd have whopped you. I often wonder what became of you too, mate. I hope that life has treated you well.

There has been a recent addition to this little story some fifty-eight years after the event. I saw a comment by Andy Millington on social media, so I replied to it.

"Are you the Andy Millington who split my lip with a superb straight jab at the old oak in the 1960s?"

"I "Err!....... I don't know. How big are you now?" came Andy's humorous reply.

Dad's Final Football Glory

Works football teams were much more popular then than today, and my Dad played for a number of them during his younger years, including Sketchley Works. He also played for his Army regiment in the late 1940s and early 1950s. He was quite a good centre-forward. Traditional positions were observed in those days. Every team played Five, Three, or Two. He was known for enthusing other players and driving them forward.

During the time I was at HHS, he worked at Oldham's Hosiery. The works team was struggling for players and needed to win an important match. He was approached and begged to fill this gap and eventually agreed. So, in his late thirties, out of training and with a bit of a pot belly, my Dad played his final match. I cannot remember why but we were about ten minutes late arriving at Queens Park. Oldham's were playing with ten men and were already a goal down.

After a brief conversation with the team manager, they caught the referee's eye, and he waved Dad onto the pitch just as the ball came across the field. Without hesitation, Dad ran straight onto it, took it all the way down the right wing, then slipped inside as he approached the goal, dodged two defenders and blasted the ball into the back of the net to equalize. There were a few frozen seconds during which we all stood open-mouthed and tried to take in what had just happened. The next second we were jumping up and down and bellowing and celebrating like mad. One – All. The rest of the match was hard fought.

We had the most possession, but they all dropped back and defended well. Towards the end of the second half, someone made a terrific cross and placed the ball just in front of Dad as he picked up speed and thundered down the pitch. His shot ricocheted off a defender, and the ball bobbed around the box with most of the players on the pitch trying to boot it either toward or away from the goal. It was mayhem. Someone chipped it in the air, and who do you think leaped up and nodded the ball past the keeper to score the winning goal? None other than my Dad. It was the decider. What a great match. I was so proud of my Dad.

He was knackered. Once home, he sat slumped in his armchair for the rest of the day. He walked like an old man for the rest of the week and moaned and groaned from his aches and pains with every movement he made. He had enjoyed his last piece of football glory, the end of his football career. They thought it was all over. It is now.

EPILOGUE

My Grandad's Big Gamble

We were in the Earl Shilton home of my paternal grandparents. I was about fourteen years old. It was a Sunday afternoon, and we had been invited for tea. Tinned salmon and lovely fresh, crunchy salad with lovely tomatoes grown by my Grandad. Endless refills of tea in beautiful bone-china cups with Grans own made fruitcake followed by tinned strawberries and cream. That's how Sunday teas were made in those days. Only when everyone had finished eating did we leave the table and make ourselves comfortable in the living room.

"So then, Raymond, how's your shop idea coming along?" asked Grandad of my Dad

"Well, not very well, if I'm honest."

"What's the trouble then."

"Well, I have done my homework, and we have looked at a dozen or more shops and found one in Hinckley that we would like to buy. The problem is that although I have saved a reasonable deposit, I would need a small business loan to buy the stock at valuation and so on, on top of a mortgage. The Bank tells me this puts the total monies borrowed outside the ratio to deposit. In a nutshell, living in a council property, I have nothing to offer in the way of collateral, so the bank is saying no to my request for a loan."
Grandad was quiet for a moment, then spoke in his quiet, deep voice

"Make another appointment at the bank Raymond but give me time to see my solicitor. Since I paid off my mortgage, he holds the deeds to my house, and you can use them as collateral for your loan."
There was a stunned silence before my Dad spoke to his Dad.

"You can't do that, Dad. If something went wrong, you could lose the roof over your head."

"I can do that, Raymond, and you won't go wrong, so make that appointment at the bank, and that's the end of it."

Although my Grandad was quietly spoken and never used bad language, he was not a man to argue with, so that, indeed, was the end of it.

Even at that age, I was just amazed at the enormity of what my Grandad had just done for my Dad. Without fuss or hesitation, consulting Gran or allowing Dad to refuse help, he made that massive decision, at huge risk to himself, to help his son. Wow!

The Shop

It must have been early 1965 that my Dad, by now established as a competent hosiery knitter, decided to raise his game further. He was earning fairly good money in the hosiery, but he had been striving to improve things for himself and the family since he had left the army. Now don't get me wrong, there is nothing wrong in living in a rented house, either council or private, but Dad wanted to own a house and felt that if he was going to buy his own home, he needed to do something now rather than later. He and Mum decided that they had the necessary skills to be able to run a shop.

Dad obeyed Grandad's instruction and kept the appointment at the bank. The bank accepted Grandad's house deeds as collateral, and Dad got his loan.

So that's how we came to be leaving Burbage. I was sorry in many ways, leaving behind many friends and all I had ever known, really. On the other hand, my best friends and I were old enough now to still visit each other from time to time. Mixed feelings of trepidation and excitement kept me awake at night during the period we began to organize our move and chase solicitors to do their stuff.

As I only had a short time left to do at Hastings High school, the Education Authority allowed me to stay there instead of moving to a new school for the sake of a couple of months. After that, I had a summer break and prepared myself to join hundreds of other youngsters at Hinckley Grammar School. It was a completely new start, and I promised myself that I would stop messing about and getting stuck in at my new school. I did too. I couldn't help but wonder then what the future might hold for a Burbage Boy named Dangerous Den.

This is what I looked like at the end of my Burbage Boyhood

I stumbled quite by chance upon a memory
A memory I stumbled upon today
And kids were playing there, just like I used to play

I pondered on those Summer hot and dusty days
And wondered where the years have all gone to
When days were long but far too short
For all we had to do

I stumbled quite by chance upon a memory
A memory that I almost forgot
I gazed upon the scene
And feel good I got

It made me realize that though the years go by
Happy kids will be there always
To bring back memories good we spent
Back in our younger days

You may say it's different now
Not how it used to be
But I don't agree
Some things don't change anyhow
Just look around and see
'Cos trees and flowers still they grow
And buds appear in spring
Birds will always sing
The same as they did long ago
Sweet memories they bring

I stumbled quite by chance upon a memory
And for the young, one day, today will be
A memory from the past and just by chance, like me
In many years to come the past, they'll stumble on
And wonder where have all the years gone to
When days were long but far too short for all they had to do

Written By Chas Hodges 1943 – 2018

Printed in Great Britain
by Amazon